How it was
in advertising : 1776~1976

Compiled by the editors of Advertising Age

CRAIN BOOKS

A Division of Crain Communications Inc.

740 RUSH STREET/CHICAGO ILLINOIS 60611

Library of Congress Catalogue Card Number: 76-203-49
ISBN 0-87251-28-X

Printed in the United States of America

776

Contents

Introduction

Although the use of advertising in extensive quantities, and particularly the development of radio and television advertising, are largely related to the last third or quarter of the Bicentennial of the United States, advertising has played an important (and often controversial role in the entire history of the country.

In an effort to record the early history of American advertising, to demonstrate its development and growth, and to provide cogent discussion of the role of advertising in American economic and social development, *Advertising Age* devoted a major portion of its special Bicentennial issue in April, 1976, to a wide variety of material dealing with advertising's history and growth.

Encouraged by the response to this effort, the editors of *Advertising Age* decided to reprint this historical material and to make it available particularly to students and teachers through the medium of college and university and school libraries.

We hope it fulfills its mission of acquainting students and educators, particularly, with a well rounded, informative picture of the role and function of advertising and its place in the first two hundred years of American history.

THE EDITORS
ADVERTISING AGE

A statement by the President

We are now marking the 200th anniversary of the American Revolution. For two centuries we have grown, changed and flourished as an independent nation. A diverse people, drawn from all corners of the earth, have joined together to fulfill the promise of democracy.

America's Bicentennial is rich in history and in the promise and potential of the years that lie ahead. It is about the events of our past, our achievements, our traditions, our diversity, our freedoms, our form of government and our continuing commitment to a better life for all Americans.

The system of free enterprise which is enjoyed as a part of our national heritage, has been effectively and capably promulgated through the various elements of the advertising media. This further evidences those values which are inherent to our American way of life.

The Bicentennial offers each of us the opportunity to join with our fellow citizens in honoring the past and preparing for the future in communities across the nation. Thus, in joining together as races, nationalities and individuals, we also retain and strengthen our traditions, background and personal freedom.

As we lay the cornerstone of America's Third Century, I am most happy to commend the publisher, editor and staff of ADVERTISING AGE on your special commemoration of our nation's 200th anniversary. Efforts such as yours are helping to make this great national celebration a memorable and meaningful one for all. #

Gerald R. Ford

How it was in advertising: 1776-1976

BY THOMAS FLEMING

Most people picture the Americans of 1776 as simple farmers struggling to survive in a primitive economy. Only when they freed themselves from British oppression did America's entrepreneurial spirit supposedly begin its great leaps forward to the abundance of 1976. With the Bicentennial year upon us, it is time to dispense with these illusions.

America in 1776 was not a puny backward nation. It was underdeveloped only in comparison with America of 1976. Its economy was already one of the most dynamic in the entire civilized world. In fact, economic historians now conclude that on a per capita basis, Americans of 1776 were the wealthiest people around.

We were already producing one-seventh of the world's iron. Our ships were hauling tons of rice and grain to Europe's hungry millions at a hefty profit for our commercial farmers. Many of these farmers, such as Robert Carter of Virginia, were also successful manufacturers, running public bakeries, textile mills and iron works. In the Connecticut factory of Simon Huntington, a single workman using water power could produce 5,000 lbs. of chocolate a year. John Adam Dagyr of Lynn, Mass., produced 80,000 pairs of shoes a year—not a bad figure for a population of 2,500,000. As early as 1767, Adino Paddock of Boston, the premiere colonial coach manufacturer, was running advertisements offering to take "old chaises in part pay for new" and regularly offered second-hand chaises "under their value" to eliminate storage charges. In spite of the fact that coach making was a luxury craft—a plain coach cost 165 pounds ($8,250 in contemporary cash) and a fancy one, 200 pounds ($10,-000)—Paddock's factory boomed.

American abundance was a fact of life, almost from the moment the first settler landed in Virginia. The richness of the land staggered everyone who saw it. The Revolution was fought not to throw off an oppressive government, but to decide who was going to control these riches—

A panoramic view of advertising in the U.S. since 1776, including the influence on it of Benjamin Franklin and its brief use by such notables as George Washington and Paul Revere, is presented by an historian in this special Bicentennial issue. Thomas Fleming, a fellow of the Society of American Historians, is author of "Now We Are Enemies," "The Man from Monticello" and "Benjamin Franklin, a Biography in His Own Words."

the Americans who were on the scene, or the British, who had only begun to glimpse the real dimensions of American prosperity. The Americans won, just barely. To their mortification, they needed immense amounts of help from France.

Patriots and politicians with guts (which are the same thing) were as scarce in 1776 as they are in 1976. Perhaps the most remarkable letter of the Revolution was written in 1777 by Charles Carroll of Carrollton, the richest man in America. It explains why it took seven years to win the war. ". . . Our people have not felt any great share of oppression under the British government. The duties collected were but trifling. . . . It will [therefore] be imprudent to tax the people to the extent of what they can even bear, and without doing it, I do not see how we shall support the war, unless some European power should assist us with money." The politicians of 1776 were as terrified of disrupting American prosperity as the politicians of 1976.

Advertising was already playing a potent role in this expanding economy. When the British and Americans opened fire on each other on April 19, 1775, during an unexpected confrontation on the town green of Lexington, Mass., there were 37 newspapers in the 13 colonies. All of them carried substantial amounts of advertising and had already reached a considerable degree of sophistication in copy and display.

Ben Franklin Spruced Up the Ads

The man behind the sophistication was also a major man behind the Revolution—Benjamin Franklin. When Franklin started his newspaper, the *Pensylvania Gazette,* in 1729, American advertising was as primitive as the plumbing. An imitation of British newspapers, it consisted of solid banks of three or four-line notices. These told us things about the society of the period, such as the remarkable number of black slaves and white indentured servants who ran away from their masters. But the ads were a trial to read. They were printed in scrambled type and uneven lines.

Franklin changed this style drastically. As one historian put it, "He opened up soggy columns by separating each advertisement from its neighbors above and below with several lines of white space. A 14-point heading for each advertisement was another innovation. At first the heading constituted the first line of the advertisement. Later it was shortened and centered, making a real heading."

Franklin's use of type was masterful. He knew instinctively what appealed to the eye. Next he began using illustrations, something not even the most advanced London printers considered. He used one and one-quarter inch cuts of ships to announce cargo and passenger space. From these he advanced to half-column and even full-column cuts made for an individual advertiser. The sign of the golden spectacles advertised one of

5

Philadelphia's leading opticians. The sign of the blue hand told the story of a reliable glove and clothing cleaner. He also created ornamental borders for clothing shops and other retail outlets, as well as cuts of scythes and sickles, clock faces, books, horses, and other symbols that instantly informed the reader about the general contents of the advertisement.

Until Franklin arrived, merchants were content with a simple announcement: "Just imported—a variety of goods." Ben taught them the value of telling their story in detail, listing in ten and 20-line ads the colors, varieties, names and sizes of the goods.

Pushing Franklin's Stove—and Soap

Franklin also advertised the family soap, which was made by two of his brothers in Boston from a formula inherited from his soapmaker father. Here is the copy he wrote for it.

"It cleanses fine linens, muslins, laces, chintzes, cambricks, etc., with ease and expedition, which often suffer more from the long and hard rubbing of the washer, through the ill qualities of the soap, than the wearing."

Franklin also advertised the stove he invented, the Pennsylvania fireplace:

"Fireplaces with small openings cause drafts or cold air to rush in at every crevice, and 'tis very uncomfortable as

The first colonial newspaper was published in Boston on Sept. 25, 1690. After one issue, it was banned by the governor, who found it objectionable.

well as dangerous to sit against any such crevice.... Women, particularly from this cause (as they sit so much in the house) get cold in the head, rheums, and defluxions which fall into their jaws and gums, and have destroyed early, many a fine set of teeth in these northern colonies. Great and bright fires do also very much contribute to damaging the eyes, dry and shrivel the skin, bring on early the appearance of old age."

More than one scholar has pointed out that many of the basic techniques of modern advertising are in that copy. Franklin sold not only his stove but the health, comfort, and pleasure to be derived from its use. He promised a miserable fate to those who ignored his product and aimed his appeal at women, more than at men, even though women did not theoretically control many purse strings in the 18th century.

Franklin's advertising rates were low by modern standards. He charged five shillings for a "moderate length" advertisement. Even granting him a 100 lines of type, which meant a crowded page, something Franklin disliked, this gave him only 20 shillings a column. With about half of his four-page paper devoted to advertisements, Franklin at best grossed 80 shillings an issue from his advertisements. Normally his gross was below this figure, since he gave lower rates to repeat advertisers. He probably averaged about 60 shillings an issue— about $250 in 1976 dollars. But his subscription price was high—10 shillings ($25) a year. It would take another century before newspaper men discovered that they could take a loss on the price of the paper and make up the difference with advertising revenue.

35% Profit on Political Pamphlets

But newspaper ads were by no means the only source of income for Benjamin Franklin and his fellow printers. They did a very brisk business in single advertisements which were pasted up on the sides of barns and houses and the doors of taverns, advertising everything from a night school to the sale of a bankrupt's household goods. Franklin also wrote and published the most successful almanac in America, printed other books, and sold thousands of imported English books which he advertised briskly in his paper. He printed speeches, paper money, political pamphlets—on all of which he averaged a 35% profit—a third higher than publishing profits in England.

He was the silent partner in the creation of a half dozen newspapers in other colonies. At the age of 42, he had an income of 2,000 pounds ($100,000) a year. Like some 20th century admen, such as

Oldest continuously published newspaper in the U.S. is the Hartford Courant. Its predecessor, the Connecticut Courant, began its publishing career in 1764.

William Benton, he retired early, handing the business over to a partner with the understanding that he would receive 50% of the profits for the next 18 years. Franklin's share came to 8,414 pounds ($420,700)—about $25,000 a year. Pretty good for a business whose operating equipment at the conclusion of the partnership was valued at only 184 pounds— about $10,000.

Franklin—and advertising—played a major role in the first British policy blunder—the attempt to impose a stamp tax on the 13 colonies in 1765. The bill taxed almost every piece of paper involved in law or commerce in America— some 55 items. But it fell with particular force on newspapers. Following the provisions of a 1712 English law, it added a surcharge of two shillings to every advertisement, and required newspapers to use only paper on which a stamp duty had been paid—which meant a higher cost for the printer. This ad tax had been a potent tool for reducing the power of the press in England, and American newspapers screamed defiance. Oddly, Franklin recommended paying the tax— pretty good evidence that American claims of inability to pay were mostly bunk. Americans in 1765 (and in 1776) were the lowest taxed people in the western world. Only when Franklin, who was living in England when the act was passed, learned that Americans were violently resisting it, did he become a prominent lobbyist for its repeal.

Paul Revere Had an Ad for It

Benjamin Franklin was not the only famous American who saw the value of advertising. Paul Revere inserted the following ad in the *Boston Gazette* for Dec. 19, 1768.

"Whereas many persons are so unfortunate as to lose their fore-teeth by accident, and otherways to their great detriment, not only in looks, but speaking both in public and private:—this is to inform all such that they may have them replaced with artificial ones that looks as well as the natural, and answers the end of speaking to all intents, by PAUL REVERE, Goldsmith, near the head of Dr. Clark's Wharf, Boston."

That well known speculator in western lands, George Washington, inserted

---

Scores first in 1704

The first paid ad in an American newspaper ran in the *Boston News Letter* on May 8, 1704. It sought a buyer or renter for an Oyster Bay, L. I., estate. There was no advertising art in newspapers until 1765. When the *Pennsylvania Packet & Advertiser* made its debut on Sept. 21, 1784, as the first daily newspaper, it ran to four pages—16 columns. Ten of the 16 columns were ads for auction sales, ship sailings and real estate availabilities.

---

an ad in the *Maryland Advocate & Commercial Advertiser* for July 15, 1773, and in the *Pennsylvania Gazette* the following September, advertising the lease of his western lands to tenant farmers (*See reproduction on Page 68, Fig. 1*). As copywriter, Washington was no Ben Franklin. His style was turgid. He never made a profit on his western lands.

Washington was a reader as well as a writer of ads. On Jan. 29, 1789, he wrote to Maj. Gen. Henry Knox in New York telling him that he had "learnt from an advertisement in the *New York Daily Advertiser* that there were superfine American broadcloths to be sold at No. 44 in Water Street." Washington was trying to encourage American manufacturing. He wore this or some other American broadcloth at his inauguration. But in the same letter he implicitly admitted that national policy had little impact on Martha. For he ordered "as much of what is called (in the advertisement) London Smoke as will make her a riding habit."

Benjamin Franklin was not the only man with advertising talent. One historian credits a merchant, Gerardus Duyckinck, as the most progressive adver-

By the middle 1800s, the typography, illustrations and copy in advertising had changed into a robust hard sell, as seen in these ads for "sulkies and sporting traps" and other vehicles of the era.

tiser in Revolutionary America. Significantly, he advertised in the *New York Post Boy*, a paper that Franklin helped found. Duyckinck used five or six inches to list a great variety of merchandise—often as many as 50 or 60 items—ranging from drugs and spices to hatters' trimmings. He employed what was probably the earliest ornamental border in advertising history—a design that imitated a carved mirror frame. Inside it his copy was printed in delicate Roman and italic faces.

More than one colonial craftsman used

advertising to attack his competition. When William Knapp discovered that Charles Willson Peale had become a rival watchmaker and repairer in Annapolis in 1768, he placed an ad in the local paper warning the public "against the continued butcheries practiced by many pretenders in the business . . . Heavy charges inevitably follow, to rectify the errors of those tinkering performers."

Doctors advertised lavishly in colonial newspapers, frequently with testimonials from cured patients to back them up.

Typical was Dr. Yeldall, who advertised in 1775 that "at his medicinal ware-house on Front Street in New York" he had almost every medicine known to science. People who lived in the country could send an account of their disorder "either in writing or otherwise" [presumably by word of mouth] and he would send them the medicine they needed. Backing up the physician was one Alexander Martin of New Jersey, who said he had been afflicted with a consumptive disorder for "upwards of three years" and had sought relief from dozens of doctors. A short course of treatment by Dr. Yeldall restored him to "perfect health."

It is clear from reading the advertisements of 1776 shopkeepers that they were appealing to a wealthy public. They offered a staggering array of dress materials: Flowered, striped, figured, and plain modes and satins in every imaginable color; equally numerous colors of damask, saracenet, and lustring, luxurious Chinese taffetas, cotton chintzes and calicoes from India and linen from Ireland and Russia. A good complexion was considered a necessity. In fact, almost every lady in Virginia wore a red cloak when abroad and muffled up her head and neck with a handkerchief, leaving only a narrow passage for the eyes. One visitor thought that everyone he met had the mumps or a toothache.

To improve the complexion or repair damage caused by the sun or wind, there were paints from China, a lip salve from India. The Bloom of Circasia "instantly gave to the cheek a rose hue not to be distinguished from the animated bloom of rural beauty." Moreover, it was guaranteed not to come off with perspiration. Other popular items were Jerusalem wash balls and "swan skin and silk powder puffs," almond paste for the hands and face, and a wide variety of perfumes, which were badly needed because frequent bathing was not in fashion.

Recruitment Ads in 1776

During the Revolution, advertising played the role it has played in all the nation's wars—it recruited men for the Army and the Navy. Above is a typical American Army recruiting ad.

In the Revolution, America's Navy consisted largely of privateers. The crew of a privateer got a cut of the profits. The copywriters made this fact the heart of the ad. A typical privateering ad began.

ALL THOSE JOLLY FELLOWS
WHO LOVE THEIR COUNTRY
AND WANT TO MAKE THEIR
FORTUNE AT ONE STROKE
REPAIR IMMEDIATELY
TO THE RENDEZVOUS
AT THE HEAD OF
HIS EXCELLENCY
GOVERNOR HANCOCK'S WHARF

Such ads explain why there were perhaps 30,000 men on the high seas privateering while Washington was having trouble scraping together 10,000 recruits for his army. As for the tiny regular American Navy, one of its civilian officials was reduced to pleading with Congress to close the ports until "the fleet is compleatly mann'd." Congress wisely ignored him. The politicians knew they had no hope of stopping the jolly fellows who were eager to make their fortunes in one stroke.

There were 43 American newspapers in business at the end of the Revolution—an increase of six, in spite of a long, exhausting war and chaotic inflation. Americans were now the dominant power on an immensely rich continent, and the rapid multiplication of population newspapers and advertising began. By 1790 there were 106 newspapers. By 1820, there were 532 papers serving a population of 9,638,000.

Unfortunately, these gross figures represent the only progress advertising can claim for this period. In style and content there was even a lamentable regression. The problem was a national paper shortage. Existing technology simply could not produce enough paper to meet the demands of multiplying newspapers and rising circulations. Editors also succumbed to the idea that the *number* of advertisments was a sign of prestige. Ads became little more than legal notices jammed into crowded columns in six-point type. Papers and their advertising remained local. Editors sold space to merchants by the year, usually for $30. A publisher could make a profit on a circulation as small as 300 copies a week.

New York's population was 125,000 in 1816. The *Mercantile Advertiser,* the largest paper, had a circulation of 2,250. The total circulation of the seven papers serving the city was 9,420, but their readership was seven or eight times that figure. Printed on rag paper, they did not wear out quickly and were available to patrons of taverns, barber shops, general stores, and other places where people socialized. Few papers were more than four pages, which practically guaranteed a merchant that even in a crowded column his five-line ad would be read.

Jefferson Had His Own Newspaper

People paid only passing attention to advertising in this era. It was considered a normal part of every newspaper. But the readers' emotions and primary interests were engaged by the editorial and news columns of the average paper, which was almost always extremely partisan. The era of objective reporting was decades away. Almost every politician—including Jefferson, Hamilton, Burr and Andrew Jackson—had his own newspaper, which laid down a party line which was more or less followed by scores of other papers. But advertising was the best reflector of the changes that were transforming America. Instead of "just imported" or "fresh importations," ads now began to stress the phrase, "American-made." Factory production of all kinds began rising at almost exponential rates. Between 1808 and 1810, it jumped from 120,000,000 units to 198,000,000 units. Textile production leaped from 8,000 spindles in 1808 to 500,000 by 1815.

First 1¢ Newspaper Is Born

Simultaneously, technology created a

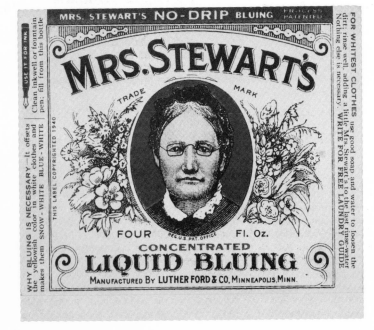

Something old, blue in 1883

Old product still found on supermarket shelves in West and Midwest is Mrs. Stewart's bluing. The label and trademark go back to 1883

publishing revolution. By 1820 advances in the chemistry of papermaking and developments in factory machinery ended the shortage and reduced the cost of paper an astonishing 25%. Editors doubled the size of their pages, although most still retained the four-page formula. For another 20 years, rivalry in page size continued until some papers reached the unwieldy spread of six feet when open. Several shrewd editors saw the idiocy of this trend. When steam-driven presses arrived in the early 1830s, the stage was set for another great leap forward. Benjamin H. Day hit the streets with a 9x12″ tabloid, the *New York Sun*, the first 1¢ newspaper. In two years it was selling 20,000 copies—making it the biggest daily newspaper in the world.

On its heels came James Gordon Bennett, founder of the *New York Herald*. In 15 months he claimed a circulation of 40,000 copies and raised his price to 2¢. Bennett was not only a great editor and reporter—he was the first philosopher of the newspaper business since Franklin. "An editor must always be with the people—think with them—feel with them —and he need fear nothing. He will always be right, always be strong—always popular—always free."

Bennett was the first to see the power of mass circulation. "Books have had their day—the theaters have had their day— the temple of religion has had its day. A newspaper can be made to take the lead of all these in the great movements of human thought and of human civilization. A newspaper can send more souls to heaven and save more from hell than all the churches or chapels in New York— besides making money at the same time."

Nothing was sacred to Bennett. He attacked everyone and everything. "The world has been humbugged long enough by spouters and talkers and conventioners and legislators." He exposed Wall St. chicanery, covered scandalous court trials, printing racy testimony verbatim. Imitators sprang up in cities across the country. The low price and the brash style created newspaper readers by the tens of thousands. Editors became rich beyond Ben Franklin's wildest dreams. William N. Swain, who made $12 a week as foreman of the *New York Sun's* composing room, founded the *Philadelphia Ledger*. In 20 years he was worth $3,000,000.

The Birth of the Want Ad

The new penny papers created new advertising. Benjamin Day of the *Sun* started a new section called "Wants" where ads could be placed at a one-time rate of 50¢. Bennett created the *Herald's* famous (his numerous critics called it infamous) Personals column. A sample:

"DEAR CHARLES—SHOULD SUCH

This recruiting ad must have had Washington's permission to use his name.

A TRIFLE AS A HANDY hat-brush sever love? Come to your ruffled LU-LU."

"MAUDE—WILL NOT BE PRUDENT FOR ME TO WRITE. I want to see you so much. LITTLE FRIEND."

"WANTED—a situation as son-in-law in a respectable family. Blood and breeding no object, being already supplied; capital essential. No objection to going a short distance into the country."

Bennett recognized that advertising could be news and he soon abandoned the prevailing custom of allowing merchants to run the same ad, day after day for years. No advertisement could appear in the *Herald* for more than two weeks. In 1848, he narrowed this rule to a single day. He also banned illustrations, guaranteeing every advertiser the same degree of attraction. Advertisers meekly submitted; the *Herald's* circulation made it impregnable to pressure. At one point, New York's theatrical managers tried to force Bennett to accept the flamboyant display advertisements of P. T. Barnum's American Museum and other attractions. When Bennett refused, they boycotted the *Herald*. Within a year, they had humbly returned.

P. T. Barnum was the man who made Americans aware of the power of advertising in its own right. With gigantic posters and ads in all available papers, he lured Americans to see everything from models of Niagara Falls to the "Fiji Mermaid" (actually the head of a monkey sewn to the body of a fish) to Tom Thumb. "I knew that every dollar sown in advertising would return in tens, and perhaps in hundreds in a future harvest," he said, looking back on his gaudy career. Barum became a hero to 19th-century advertising men. But he was a dangerous model. Too much of what he advertised was fake.

Less well known but even more successful, with more exclusive dependence on advertising (much of what Barnum called advertising we would call publicity) was Robert Bonner of the *New York Ledger*. In the 1850s, he transformed this ex-trade journal into a "literary paper" —a kind of pulp magazine with a circulation of 400,000, an impressive figure in a country whose total population was only 51,000,000. Bonner accepted no advertising in the *Ledger*. But he spent as much as $27,000 in one week to advertise it elsewhere. With sheer ingenuity he broke through James Gordon Bennett's prohibitions against display advertising. He took columns, and finally whole pages of the *Herald* in which he wrote copy like this:

THE NEW YORK LEDGER
THE NEW YORK LEDGER
THE NEW YORK LEDGER
WILL BE FOR SALE
WILL BE FOR SALE
WILL BE FOR SALE
TOMORROW MORNING
TOMORROW MORNING
TOMORROW MORNING
THROUGHOUT THE UNITED STATES
THROUGHOUT THE UNITED STATES
THROUGHOUT THE UNITED STATES
AND NEW JERSEY
AND NEW JERSEY
AND NEW JERSEY

Sometimes Bonner bought a whole page in the *Herald*, which simply repeated a single ad 93 times.

By this time there were 3,000 publications reaching American readers. Weekly newspapers still dominated the field— there were 2,300 of them vs. 200 dailies. The major New York papers, notably the *Herald* and the *Tribune*, issued weeklies which had national circulations of as much as 100,000. Magazines—there were over 500 of them—still shunned advertising and newspapers maintained their prejudice against display advertising.

But there was emerging on the publishing scene a man who would soon transform these conservative fixations: The advertising agent. His arrival was almost inevitable. The system cried out for a middle man.

There was a bewildering variety of newspapers and magazines on one side, and on the other side an equally bewildering variety of merchants and manufacturers with no easy way of discovering each other. A man making a product with a national sales potential had no way of finding out how many newspapers there were in Dubuque, much less which one was the best, without sending himself or one of his executives there. The advertising agent filled this vacuum by supplying the business man with lists of papers and the papers with ads for their hungry pages.

The First Agency Man Gets 25%

It may not be relevant to the big historical picture, but it is interesting to note that the first advertising agent went mad. His name was Volney B. Palmer, and he began his career, like most agents, as an advertising solicitor for a local paper. He switched to selling space for a string of country newspapers, and soon had offices in Philadelphia, Boston and New York. Plump and pompous, he wore gold-rimmed spectacles and carried a gold-headed cane. One of his proteges, S. M. Pettingill, said, "He had more self possession and assurance than any man I ever knew."

When Pettingill set up his own agency, Palmer's reaction more than equaled the fury which similar moves often elicit on modern Madison Ave. Palmer wrote every important newspaper in the country, warning them that Pettingill was a fraud. But the newspapers were delighted to break the brief monopoly which Palmer enjoyed. Palmer had aroused the wrath of more than one editor by insisting on a 25% commission for all the advertising that appeared in any newspaper he represented.

By the time the Civil War began there were about 20 advertising agents in New York and 10 operating in other cities. They all made plenty of money. Newspapers had so-called rate cards. But no sensible agent paid much attention to them. A shrewd bargainer could beat a cash-short editor down to 10% of his standard price. He also frequently doubled his 25% commission. But he could also lose the business the following week to someone offering a better deal. Such chaos was not particularly good for human nervous systems and may explain why Volney B. Palmer wound up babbling to a keeper hired by Horace Greeley.

S. M. Pettingill was meanwhile creating another first—he began writing copy for one of his advertisers, a clothing store named Oak Hall. Commissioned to write an ad a day, the straining Pettingill resorted to doggerel. He signed some of it "Prof. Littlefellow," and then "Prof.

Shortfellow." Finally he signed one "Prof. Longfellow." This drew a ferocious protest from Cambridge, where the poet of the same name was reigning as America's chief historical mythmaker. Advertising's first celebrity endorsement vanished under the threat of a lawsuit.

Ads Help Civil War Bonds Sell Big

The Civil War soon produced advertising's first national success story. Advertising agent L. F. Shattuck was selected by financier Jay Cooke to market the government's war loans. Shattuck placed ads in some 5,000 publications at card rates, and the bond issue was a stupendous success Advertising, wrote a pundit in 1867, was the monomania of the times. It was only 0.1% of the volume it has reached today. But the American century, which began a few years after the Civil War, when the U.S. seized the industrial leadership of the world from Great Britain, was on its way.

Inevitably the advertising jungle soon acquired a king. He was George P. Rowell, a New Hampshire farm boy who began as an ad solicitor in Boston. He added stability with a new idea. He bought up space in over 100 papers and offered it to advertisers on a contract basis. Rowell also guaranteed payment of any ad for which he received a commission. Other agents took their commissions and let the publishers worry about collecting the rest of the money. Rowell also

1914

1923

10

The first magazine ad for the first contour bottle of Coke advertised it as the "master drink in the master bottle." The contour bottle shape long ago was granted trademark status and today it is registered with the U.S. Patents & Trademark office.

1894-1899   1900-1916   1916-1956   1956-1976

Named for designer, "Hutchinson" Coke bottle (left) gave "pop" nickname to soft drinks. To open, you pushed wire and rubber stopper into bottle. A loud "pop" then was heard.

stopped bargaining with publishers on commissions, allowing "usage" to create "an established per cent"—usually 25%.

In 1869 Rowell published the first American newspaper directory, giving publishers at least an estimate of each newspaper's circulation. He was threatened with libel suits by the dozen, because almost all publishers used inflated figures. But no one sued him. Rowell also founded *Printer's Ink* in 1888.

By this time, he was a very rich man and the first philosopher of advertising. "Advertising," he wrote, "is publicity, a means of causing it to be known what service you or I can render, what wants we can satisfy, and the reasons why that service should be sought at our hands." Rowell also candidly admitted the central problem of all advertising then and now: "As a general thing, the advertiser cannot tell whether a particular advertisement pays him or not."

At the same time, Rowell revealed a curious mental anomaly, shared by almost all the advertising agents of his era. In an essay entitled "The Principles of Advertising," he wrote, "Honesty is by all odds the very strongest point which can be crowded into an advertisement."

Yet Rowell made almost all his money from advertising patent medicines. So did most other advertising agents. Patent medicines and quack doctor ads had been advertising staples since Ben Franklin's day. But after the Civil War the medicines and the ads for them reached deluge proportions. Some people blamed it on the impaired health of the Civil War soldiers. Others blamed it on advertising. Owning a patent medicine was a quick way to make a fortune and Rowell, along with numerous other agents, owned several nostrums with no health value whatsoever.

Was Adman 'a Respectable Crook?'

In his memoirs, Rowell puzzled over one of the first uses of a mystery formula, "S.T.1860X," which was a basic part of all ads for Plantation Bitters, one of the big sellers of the day. Rowell thought it meant "Started trade in 1860 with ten

1956

An early automobile, Dodge came out in 1914 with a 110-inch wheelbase model, as the ads listed such things as "shipping weight 2200 lbs" and "radiator—tubular type." Price: $785. In 1923, the selling point was "strength and safety" of a steel body, while 33 years later, the 1956 Dodge was the "value leader of the forward look."

dollars capital." But the owner of the concoction told him that it meant nothing at all. "Such combinations do come to have an advertising value," Rowell wrote, "as is evidenced by the three Rs of Radways Ready Relief, the three Ss of Swift's Syphilitic Specific, and the C.C.C. of Cascarets Candy Cathartic."

The naked admiration which advertising men like Rowell expressed for the patent medicine tycoons—the owner of Hostetters Bitters left a fortune of $18,-000,000—and the public knowledge that advertising men were frequently involved as owners as well as promoters of patent medicines gave advertising an unsavory reputation. One business man told the dignified Daniel M. Lord, who founded Lord & Thomas, that an advertising man was no more than a respectable crook.

The still superficial role of the agent also made it hard for many business men to take advertising seriously. F. Wayland Ayer, founder of N. W. Ayer & Son, winced when an aristocratic Philadelphia friend remarked that he admired him for his personal qualities, but he could never have any respect for Ayer as a business man. "What is an advertising agent?" he asked, "Nothing but a drummer and he never will be anything else."

The insult stung Ayer into giving some serious thought to the advertising business. He admitted there was some truth to the sneer. He vowed to change the situation. "I will not be an order taker any longer . . . I will have clients rather than people who just give me orders."

Ayer saw that George Rowell's attempt to stabilize the business was unsuccessful. Rowell left too much to "usage" in creating an established percentage for a commission. Moreover, the advertiser had to take Rowell's word for what had been established. Although Rowell claimed to represent the advertiser, he still got his money from the publishers, and there was too much room for an unscrupulous agent to enlarge his take indefinitely. So ad agents had a reputation as sharpsters.

Ayer's answer was the open contract, which clearly stated that the agent represented the advertiser and stipulated how much money would be spent, plus a commission of 12.5%, which was soon raised to 15%. The open contract did not resolve the conflict about where the advertising agent's fees come from. The issue is still being debated—along with rate cutting and split commissions—today. But it did produce a massive shift in the gravity of the advertising business, tipping most agents toward the advertiser as his representative.

From that shift soon flowed the concept of servicing the advertiser in various ways, from studying the market to writing copy for his ads. Within four years

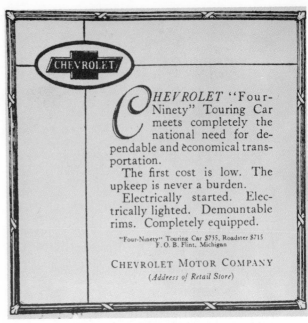

1919

The first ad for Chevrolet appeared in May, 1919, promoting a "Four Ninety" touring car for $735. In 1927, Campbell-Ewald termed that year's model "the most beautiful Chevrolet in Chevrolet history," with the coach model priced at $645, and the roadster at $525. By 1949, the car was being billed as "the most beautiful buy of all."

of the introduction of the open contract in 1875, Ayer took a big account for threshing machines away from George P. Rowell by producing the first marketing survey.

JWT: 'No One Else Will Make as Much'

Meanwhile, advertising had found a new medium. J. Walter Thompson had persuaded American magazines to open their pages to ads. Like George Rowell, Thompson scored an initial coup by buying up all the available space and selling it not only to advertisers but to other advertising agents, doubling his commissions. As late as 1898, Thompson continued to control all the space in most of the women's magazines as well as in the general monthlies. "No one will ever make as much money out of advertising as I have," Thompson said. With advertising revenues to support them, and postal rates legislated low for them by Congress, magazines began making quantum leaps in circulation. The *Century* was the first big success. It was soon outstripped by *Harper's*. By 1899, this magazine was carrying 135 pages of class advertising and 163 pages of editorial. But these old-line magazines were soon supplanted by new mass magazines aimed at larger circulation. As the century turned, the *Cosmopolitan, Ladies' Home Journal, Munsey's* and *McClure's* surged

past *Harper's*. The reigning genius and owner of several of these new advertising media was Cyrus H. K. Curtis.

At the same time, outdoor advertising began to burgeon. The first electric sign rose on Broadway in 1891 and the street was soon "the Great White Way," the eighth wonder of the world. To meet the competition, newspapers had long since dropped their ban on display advertising. The breakthrough in this field came from France, when French newspapers succumbed to demands from Paris department stores. In New York and Philadelphia, merchants like John Wanamaker soon made advertising the focus of their merchandising philosophy.

Men like Wanamaker did not write their own copy. They hired gifted writers. But most of these early copywriters operated independently of advertising agents. The first of these now legendary figures was John E. Powers, who got his start in England where he was a sensational success at selling sewing machines. He specialized in terse copy, often only a single line. He also had a penchant for telling the truth. One of his ads read: "We have a lot of rotten gossamers [raincoats] and things we want to get rid of." The supply was sold out in one morning. When Powers began telling the public more of the truth than Wanamaker wanted them to know, he was fired.

1927

1949

The copywriter as he functions today emerged first in Chicago under Albert D. Lasker of Lord & Thomas. For a salary of $28,000 a year, he hired John E. Kennedy, a mustachioed ex-Mountie who was writing copy for Dr. Shoop's Restorative. Kennedy's message, which Lasker spread like gospel, was simple, it seems now, to the point of brainlessness. Advertising, he said, was "salesmanship in print." To Kennedy, this meant long, convincing spiels. The era of the slogan, the one-line ad was over. The idea tripled the billings of Lord & Thomas, and Lasker was on his way to making $60,000,000. From Kennedy he progressed to another copywriter, Claude Hopkins, whose magic formula was "the reason why." Lasker preached this as a new gospel and again billings soared. Most of the time, Hopkins' reason had as much basis in reality as the claims of the patent medicines. He made Puffed Wheat and Puffed Rice national breakfasts with the claim that they were "shot from guns." But Lasker and his copywriters had an enormous impact on advertising. Before them, advertising was largely the art of buying the best available space at the cheapest rates. After them, copy was the crucial thing.

Spotlights on the Billboards

The period between 1900 and World War I has been called the golden age of

advertising. N. W. Ayer collared the first $1,000,000 account and launched the first national campaign—for Uneeda biscuit —using newspapers, magazines and outdoor advertising. The first auto ads appeared. By 1914 the car makers were spending $4,000,000 a year. Advertising was ubiquitous. At night, the Hudson River steamboats to Albany turned on their searchlights so the passengers could read the billboards lining the banks. The country became advertising conscious. The *Atlantic Monthly* and the *Yale Review* ran articles on the subject, declaring it to be the most conspicuous feature of American life. They worried about its effect on the morals, taste and health of the nation.

Other writers did more than worry. The muckrakers, as they came to be known, unleashed a ferocious attack on phony advertising, starting with patent medicines. Next came exposés of fraudulent financial advertising. For the first time, newspapers and magazines began censoring their advertising pages. In 1910, Cyrus H. K. Curtis published the Curtis Advertising Code which declared its intention "to protect both our advertisers and our readers from all copy that is fraudulent or deceptive." Advertising executives, acting through the Advertising Federation of America, drew up a code and lobbied a model statute against

false advertising through the legislatures of some 37 states. In 1914, the newspaper division of the Associated Advertising Clubs of the World produced "Standards of Newspaper Practice." In the same year, the Adult Bureau of Circulations was born. Advertising was on the laborious path to respectability.

More than one advertiser has waxed nostalgia for the wacky, unethical good old days of the golden age. In her book, "It's an Act," Helen Woodward recalled the Ben Hampton Agency, where "everything was eager and noisy from morning till night. We had three departments, and they got all mixed up with each other.

"Everyone ran, everyone argued, everyone dashed to the telephone. We had no research department. Nobody ever dreamed of looking anything up because nothing had ever happened before. There were no records showing what other advertisers had spent. There were just a lot of people with astute and ingenious minds putting something over on the public and having an exciting and pretty good time doing it."

After World War I, advertising Charlestoned into the 1920s, a period which rates the title of silver, if not golden, age. The advertising man and the salesman shared the spotlight as national heroes. Few on Madison Ave. paid much attention to Albert Lasker's skilful use of ad-

The Cook of Spotless Town you see
Who takes the cake as you'll agree.
She holds it in her fingers now.
It isn't light - but anyhow
'Twill lighten her domestic woe -
A cake of plain

SAPOLIO

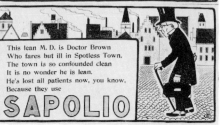

This brilliant man walks up and down
Upon the streets of Spotless Town.
The glitter of his shining star
Arrests attention from afar.
It lights the beat and goes to show
That naught can beat

SAPOLIO

This lean M. D. is Doctor Brown
Who fares but ill in Spotless Town.
The town is so confounded clean
It is no wonder he is lean.
He's lost all patients now, you know,
Because they use

SAPOLIO

Rub – a dub dub,
Three men in a tub,
They are off on a cruise
For this excellent grub.

Campbell's CONDENSED SOUPS
"Just add hot water and serve"
6 plates 10c.

Transit ads date to 1850

Transit advertising in the U. S. dates to 1850, when the first advertising "sign" appeared for Lord & Taylor on New York City's horse-drawn streetcars. By 1860, panel and frame displays appeared inside the cars, and by the 1880s, card ad advertising took on a neat appearance with the installation of uniform display racks along the walls of vehicles.

By 1890, there were attempts to organize the car card medium on a national level, and in 1893, Barron Collier, one of the great names in the transit advertising field, first tried to standardize it.

Some of the earliest transit advertisers included Campbell's soup, Wrigley's chewing gum and Sapolio. Today—with transit advertising appearing inside buses, subway cars and commuter trains, and on the outsides of such vehicles, as well—the medium has a volume of $75,000,000. #

vertising to defeat Woodrow Wilson's plea for the League of Nations. They were too busy fighting the great cigaret and soap wars, with Lasker and George Washington Hill leading the Lucky Strike brigade, paying copywriters bonuses of as much as $10,000 for a single socko slogan such as "So round, so firm, so fully packed, so free and easy on the draw." Advertisers, like other business men, congratulated themselves for prosperity, which was supposed to last forever. A new medium, radio, helped swell billings to $3.4 billion in 1929.

Consumerism Rears Its Head

Then came the Great Crash. Billings dropped a shuddering $2 billion. It would take 17 years to crawl back to the 1929 heights. While struggling to stay alive, advertising had to fight a new, much more dangerous foe than the muckrakers of the turn of the century—the consumer movement. These people did not simply demand advertising reform. They were out to abolish advertising. A parade of books, spearheaded by the best-seller, "100 Million Guinea Pigs," denounced advertising and the profit system.

Even more ominous was the entrance of the politicians. The Roosevelt Brain Trust began prescribing drastic remedies to cure advertising's supposed ills. The climax was the Wheeler-Lee Amendment of 1938 which immensely broadened the power of the Federal Trade Commission to police advertising. Other critics, such as historian Henry Steele Commager, lined up to accuse advertising of doing everything from causing academic distrust of business to interfering with normal psychological growth to picturing American society as "a nightmare of fear and jealousy, gossip and slander, envy and ambition." Even as Prof. Commager wrote these words in 1950, a new medium, television, was exploding across America, giving advertisers unparalleled power to influence the thoughts and feelings of the average man and woman.

By this time, advertising—and the rest of the economy—was back on its feet, beginning the longest, most dizzying leap forward in American history. Business had pumped millions of surplus dollars into advertising during World War II. It paid off in an unprecedented demand for postwar products and services. Advertising's growth was spectacular, with television the new champion, revolutionizing everything from sales pitches to politics, transforming radio and magazines into different media. But success only temporarily silenced advertising's critics. The upheavals of the 1960s triggered the rise of a new, more aggressive consumer movement and tougher government regulation. Advertising responded with an

other round of self policing climaxed by the creation in 1971 of the National Advertising Review Board.

Tool of Abundance, Scarcity to Come

On the philosophical level, advertising's answer to its critics has been a reiteration of its contribution to America's ever-expanding economy. This argument has been in constant use since Prof. Neil Borden of Harvard stated it in 1942. Sixteen years later, an historian of advertising proudly quoted Yale Prof. David Potter's description of advertising as "distinctively the institution of abundance." But the writer had obviously never read Potter's entire book, "People of Plenty: Economic Abundance and the American Character." Potter's thesis is the point with which this brief history began. Americans have had an economy of abundance for over 200 years. Advertising undoubtedly played a part in multiplying this abundance. But that is no longer so pertinent; a new problem confronts the American of 1976: Scarcity.

A nation of 230,000,000 is being forced to face the fact that natural resources are limited, and access to raw materials in other countries may soon require impossible financial or political sacrifices. Shortages of oil and gasoline have already drastically altered the automobile industry, to name only one primary source of advertising dollars.

What role will advertising play in an economy which no longer has riches for sale? That is the unprecedented question which advertising men—and the American people—may soon have to face.

One thing is certain. Advertising will not disappear. A business that projects billings of $30 billion for 1976 has obviously achieved status. Advertising has become a basic part of the way the American economy operates. Nor would it be overoptimistic to predict that advertising can meet the challenge of scarcity and the no-growth philosophy which some muddle-headed idealists have concocted from it.

Looking back to the patent medicine days, the pages of crowded type in the newspapers of the early 1800s, advertising men might justly select as their Bicentennial theme a variation on that slogan about coming a long way. It may make it easier to face the fact that like the rest of America, they also have a long way to go. #

ADVERTISING EVALUATION POLICY STATEMENT

NATIONAL ADVERTISING REVIEW BOARD

The National Advertising Review Board is charged by business primarily to achieve and sustain high standards of truth and accuracy in national and regional advertising.

The principal means of carrying out this mandate of self-regulation shall be through the established procedures for panels convened to adjudicate cases of alleged abuse of truth and accuracy.

In the evaluation process advertising will be reviewed in terms of its technical and literal accuracy, and thorough consideration will be given to the question of whether it has the capacity to deceive, by commission or by material omission, the potential customer who would be exposed to the advertising in question.

The issues which come before NARB panels may take a variety of forms:

The adequacy of substantiation, including research data, to support an objective claim for a product or service.

A testimonial involving the competency of the testifier as a regular user reflecting average experience.

A claim with respect to bargain or price savings for a product or service.

The matter of fair and honest reference to a competitor or of a comparison of products.

Substantiation for guarantees and warranties and whether there is adequate disclosure of pertinent information about these.

Advertising directed to children where representations not misleading to the adult mind could have the capacity to confuse or mislead the immature and impressionable mind.

These are cited here for illustrative purposes only, and each case will be decided on its own merits.

The Review Board recognizes the existence of various codes and guidelines in advertising which may be currently in use by segments of industry, and which are based on their past experience in evaluating advertising acceptability. The Council of Better Business Bureaus has developed an extensive body of precedents in this area which is available to its National Advertising Division in carrying out its staff role of initial evaluation and review.

In cases submitted to panels of the Review Board, detailed standards utilized within industry, or government decisions may be viewed as precedents for an NAD decision in a given case. The panels will consider the applicability of such standards or decisions to these cases, but are not bound by them.

Further, the executive director shall make available to NARB panels decisions rendered by previous panels for the assistance and guidance that these previous decisions may provide.

In all cases, NARB panels will seek to arrive at a fair and speedy resolution of the issues.

Recognizing that from time to time NARB will be asked to consider content of advertising messages in controversy for reasons other than truth and accuracy, the Chairman shall appoint 5-member panels from the membership whose responsibility shall be to review broad areas of concern to the public and to business involving advertising, but not relating to specific cases involving truth and accuracy.

These Panels shall consider such matters as are referred to them by the Chairman, and shall report their conclusions to the Board in writing. The Chairman shall release reports based upon the judgments of these panels and which are approved for publication by majority vote of the Board.

This distinction in evaluating advertising complaints recognizes the educational and persuasive role of NARB with respect to advertising practices in general, while at the same time acknowledging that enforcement recommendations are limited to matters of truth and accuracy.

Adopted January 20, 1972

A policy statement of the National Advertising Review Board tells what issues come before the board and what it does about them.

George Washington: advertiser

BY A. STANLEY KRAMER

To those of us who learned at an early age that George Washington was "first in peace and first in the hearts of his countrymen," it may come as somewhat of a surprise to learn that he was one of the first in American advertising as well. Washington not only wrote several advertisements, including one lengthy offering of real estate (which he had not yet seen at the time), he permitted the use of his name as an inducement in government advertising, and responded to a New York newspaper by ordering merchandise by mail from Virginia.

Advertising in colonial days was by handbill, poster and newspaper. It was vital and energetic, seeking its rewards directly and unconcerned with long-range benefits such as the creation of a brand image. Nor did these early ads consciously play on the hidden wellsprings of human behavior. Almost naively, advertisers said what they meant, and meant what they said. They offered products or services for sale, posted rewards for strayed servants and used the papers as a rented pulpit from which to address larger groups than could be assembled in a tavern.

In a single issue of a local colonial weekly the following might be found for sale: Entertainment in the form of wild beasts or clowns, dancing lessons, false teeth, medicine, sugar, tea, rum, cotton, wool, flour, fish, pitch, indigo, sole leather English steel, long and short pipes, cordage and hardware.

While we know Benjamin Franklin as a tireless advertiser, proficient copy writer and multifaceted champion of the printed word, it is rather surprising to find the austere and dignified Father of Our Country seeking "customers," as in the advertisement from stately Mt. Vernon in 1773. (See Fig. 1.)

A. Stanley Kramer, author of this story, is a Chicago promotion/adman and history buff.

In an attempt to draw settlers to his western lands, Washington wrote this ad and inserted it in the *Maryland Advocate & Commercial Advertiser* for July 15, 1773, and reran it in the *Pennsylvania Gazette* of September of that year.

It was certainly what the trade would call today "a solid pitch" playing up all the right inducements: Luxuriance of the soil, convenience to river transportation, abundance of fish and fowl, no down payment, the inevitable rise in value if a

Soldiers in colonial times were seen like this in recruiting ads, with such copy as in Fig. 2, above, right.

new government is established, and the urge to act now, before Oct. 1, so that there will be enough lots.

Despite the foregoing, and as with all too many good ads since, the results were disappointing. Few settlers responded. And ten years later when he finally visited his property, he found it occupied by squatters. Even worse, land agents ignoring his patents were selling it freely!

■ The first known use of advertising by the new government was during the American Revolution, with handbills and posters calculated to bring men into the armed services. In 1776, there were many such, offering bounties of money, clothes and farm land to those who would sign up until the end of the war. George Washington was so popular that his name was prominently featured as an inducement.

On page 9 of this book, Thomas Fleming reproduces the heading of a poster urging men to join the "troops now raising under George Washington." The text that went under that heading is reproduced at right (Fig. 2). The text (taken from "The Story of Advertising," Page 59, by James Playsted Wood (Ronald Press) was widely distributed throughout the colonies by Congress. Spaces were left blank for filling in the names of the local recruiting officers, dates and places. Because of the featured billing of Washington on the poster, it seems reasonable to assume that he was aware not only of its existence, but of the promises made, even though he was not the author.

The illustrations beneath the heading show a cockaded soldier in knee breeches going through the prescribed fourteen positions of the manual of arms. (One is reproduced here, below.)

The sufferings of the Continental Army at Valley Forge were certainly never anticipated by Washington or Congress. In unquestioned good faith they had promised the cash, "cloathing" and "the opportunity of spending a few happy years in viewing the different parts of this beautiful continent."

Unlike many advertisers who blithely shrug off the discrepancy between their product and its advertising, Washington tried his utmost to improve the horrible conditions of his men. And in a series of letters written in his own hand to Congress, he pleaded the urgency of their cause. A particularly moving letter is currently on display in the Museum of Valley Forge.

Washington was a regular reader of newspaper advertising, both local and from other cities. On Jan. 29, 1789, he wrote to Major General Henry Knox from Virginia for some cloth he had seen advertised in New York (*see illustration beginning, "My Dear Sir"*).

16

FIGURE 1 — Mount Vernon in Virginia, July 15, 1773

The subscriber having obtained patents for upwards of TWENTY THOUSAND acres of Land in the *Ohio* and *Grand Kanhawa* (Ten Thousand of which are situated on the banks of the first-mentioned river, between the mouths of the two Kanhawas and the remainder on the *Great Kanhawa* or New River, from the mouth or near it, upwards in one continued survey) proposes to divide the same into any sized tenements that may be desired, and lease them upon moderate terms, allowing a reasonable number of years rent free, provided within the space of two years from next October three acres for every fifty contained in each lot, and proportionately for a less quantity, shall be cleared, fenced, and tilled; and that by or before the time limited for the commencement of the first rent, five acres for every hundred, and proportionately as above, shall be enclosed and laid down in good grass for meadow; and moreover that at least fifty good fruit trees for every like quantity of land shall be planted on the premises. Any persons inclined to settle on these lands may be more fully informed of the terms by applying to the subscriber, near *Alexandria*, or in his absence to Mr. LUND WASHINGTON, and would do well in communicating their intentions before the 1st of October next, in order that a sufficient number of lots may be laid off to answer the demand.

As these lands are among the first which have been surveyed in the part of the country they lie in, it is amost needless to premise that none can exceed them in luxuriance of soil or convenience of situation, all of them lying upon the banks either of the Ohio or Kanhawa and abounding with fine fish and wild fowl of various kinds, also in most excellent meadows, many of which (by the bountiful hand of nature) are, in their present state, almost fit for the scythe.

From every part of these lands water carriage is now had to Fort Pitt, by an easy communication, and from Fort Pitt, up the Monongahela to Redstone, vessels of convenient burden, may and do pass continually; from whence, by means of Cheat River and other navigable branches of the Monongahela, it is thought the portage to Powtowmack may, and will, be reduced within the compass of a few miles, to the great ease and convenience of the settlers in transporting the produce of their lands to market.

To which may be added that, as patents have now actually passed the seals for the several tracts here offered to be leased, settlers on them may cultivate and enjoy the lands in peace and safety, notwithstanding the unsettled counsels respecting a new colony on the Ohio; and, as no right money is to be paid for these lands, and quitrent of two shillings sterling a hundred demandable some years hence only, it is highly presumable that they will always be held upon a more desirable footing than where both these are laid on with a very heavy hand.

And it may not be amiss further to observe that if the scheme for establishing a new government on the Ohio, in the manner talked of, should ever be effected, these must be among the most valuable lands in it, not only on account of the goodness of the soil and the other advantages above enumerated but from their contiguity to the seat of government, which more than probably will be fixed at the mouth of the Great Kanhawa.

George Washington[8]

[8] *The Writings of George Washington, from the Original Manuscript Sources.* Ed. John C. Fitzpatrick (Washington: U.S. Government Printing Office, 1931), III, 144-46.

FIGURE 2

THAT tuesday, Wednesday, Thursday, friday and Saturday at Spotswood in Middlesex Lieutenant Recruiting with his music and recruiting party [indecipherable] in the name of Major Shutes Battalion of the 11th regiment of infantry, commanded by Lieutenant Colonel Aaron Ogden for the purpose of receiving the enrollment of such youth of spirit as may be willing to enter into this HONOUR-ABLE service.

The ENCOURAGEMENT at this time to enlist, is truly liberal and generous, namely a bounty of twelve dollars, an annual and fully sufficient supply of good and handsome cloathing, a daily allowance of large and ample ration of provisions, together with SIXTY dollars a year in GOLD and SILVER money on account of pay, the whole of which the soldier may lay up for himself and friends, as all articles proper to his subsistence and comfort are provided by law, without any expence to him.

Those who may favour this recruiting party with their attendance as above, will have an opportunity of hearing and seeing in a more particular manner, the great advantages which these brave men will have, who shall embrace this opportunity of spending a few happy years in viewing the different parts of this beautiful continent, in the honourable and truly respectable character of a soldier, after which he may, if he pleases return home to his friends, with his pockets FULL of money and his head covered with laurels.

GOD SAVE THE UNITED STATES

FIGURE 3 — Mount Vernon,

My Dear Sir:

Having learnt from an Advertisement in the New York Daily Advertiser, that there were superfine American Broad Cloths to be sold at No. 44 in Water Street; I have ventured to trouble you with the Commission of purchasing enough to make me a suit of cloaths. As to the colour, I shall leave it altogether to your taste; only observing that if the dye should not appear to be well fixt & clear, or if the cloth should not really be very fine, then (in my judgment) some colour mixed in grain might be preferable to an indifferent (stained) dye. I shall have occasion to trouble you for nothing but the cloth & twist to make the button holes.

If these articles can be procured and forwarded in a package by the stage in any short time your attention will be gratefully acknowledged. Mrs. Washington would be equally thankful to you for purchasing for her use as much of what is called (in the Advertisement) London Smoke as will make her a riding habit. If the choice of these clothes should have been disposed of in New York where could they be had from Hartford in Connecticut where I perceive a Manufactory of them is established? With every sentiment of sincere friendship

I am always Affectionately Yrs.,
G. Washington

■ There is reason to believe that Washington had a more important purpose in mind than merely obtaining these small quantities of cloth for his personal use. For at all times he was eager to encourage native American industry.

Later the same year he visited the Hartford Woolen Manufacty and ordered enough "Everlasting" cloth for breeches for his male servants. This factory was operated by an old comrade-in-arms, Jeremiah Wadsworth, formerly commissary general of the Continental Army, and, obviously, a man with a sharp eye for publicity.

For on Jan. 20, 1790, an item in the *Hampshire Gazette* proudly announced: "President Washington, when he addressed the two houses of Congress on the 8th instant, was dressed in a crow colored suit of clothes of American manufacture. This elegant fabric was from the manufactory in Hartford." #

National vs. retail: The long struggle

BY S. R. BERNSTEIN

The Great Atlantic & Pacific Tea Co. has been beset with problems in recent years and has lost much of its glamor as a merchandising leader. But its long history is a saga of modern marketing in America. A&P had its beginnings in 1859 in the belief of a young Maine merchant that he could simplify the involved and tortuous distribution route through which tea from the Orient moved on its way to the New York housewife, and thus reduce the price of this commodity. His fundamental concept of simplified and more efficient distribution was so sound that George H. Hartford's tea shop on

Along with liberty and democracy, the nation was founded on capitalism. Despite its occasional creakings and resultant modifications, and whatever the new pitfalls ahead, it has succeeded brilliantly in the past 200 years. What has helped make the feat possible has been mass production and mass distribution on hitherto unheard of scale. Here is a fascinating account of the early beginnings and later development of mass distribution and its handmaidens: Retail and national advertising.

Vesey St. in New York grew steadily into today's vast producing and distributing organization.

"Americans have more of the good things of life than can be had in any other part of the world," A&P proudly told its employe family in 1959, when it celebrated its 100th birthday. "We earn more, spend more and have more because of the system under which we live. All of this is possible because we have learned two important things:

"1. The art of mass production, which means growing and manufacturing in such tremendous quantities that the cost of producing them is low.

"2. The art of mass distribution, which means getting those goods into the hands of consumers with a minimum of waste and expense."

A&P's role in mass distribution, the essential complement to mass production, is easy to assess and to understand. Its role in physically distributing the grocery and household products it produces itself and buys from other producers is clear, and familiar to all.

Getting Mass Distribution with Flair

But one potent element in A&P's great success was its early recognition of the fact that mass distribution involves more than merely having goods available for sale at convenient locations and at fair prices. It involves *communication* of these facts to the public, and development or enhancement of active demand for them. Thus, George Hartford not only sought to bring goods into the hands of consumers with a minimum of waste, but he did it "with such a merchandising flair that his single store became one of the best known and best patronized tea houses in the city."

"To bring the highest possible volume of customers marching through his store," his successors explained proudly, "he employed promotional techniques that were regarded as spectacular even in the era when P. T. Barnum was at the height of his lapel-grabbing glory. The Vesey St. store was a wonder to behold. Outside, a huge gaslit T illuminated a storefront of 'real Chinese vermilion and flaked gold.' Inside, the red and gold scheme was carried over to the numberless huge tea bins

Not only physical distribution of grocery goods with a minimum of waste, but merchandising them with flair was the mark of the early A&P, beginning in 1859 and continuing in this 1927 b&w full page in the Ladies' Home Journal.

The illustrator of the A&P magazine ad above was the then well known McClelland Barclay. The ad ran in 1927. Ad at right was the first chain grocery ad ever to appear in a national publication. After pioneering modern distribution methods, A&P was aiming at "good will."

which lined the walls; Japanese lanterns and brilliant gaslit chandeliers that threw a bright hue over the cashier's cage which was built in the shape of a Chinese pagoda and, on Saturday nights over a genuine brass band that banged out the tunes of the day . . .

"He was soon spreading his activities beyond the confines of 31 Vesey St. Advertisements began appearing in national magazines such as *Harper's Weekly* announcing the fantastic tea values available by mail order from New York; 'tea clubs' were being organized in cities up and down the coast."

Although there is no indication that James Walter Thompson had anything to do with this early A&P advertising, he most certainly would have applauded it. Mr. Hartford was, as Thompson would have put it, "reaching the millions"— making use of "another economic force that would effect a revolution in selling in the same way that Watt's steam engine revolutionized manufacturing.

"That force was advertising."

Building Trust Was Key to Success

Closely related as the A&P and the Thompson agency have been in the development of mass marketing and mass distribution, and complementary as their developments have been, they also have been major protagonists on opposing sides in an internecine warfare for dominance on the marketing scene. The young tea merchant from Maine operated in the tradition of the great early retailers like Wanamaker and Field; they built solid and substantial reputations as the purchasing agents of the American family, and Mrs. Consumer bought their wares in confidence because they stood behind them and because she trusted them and their clerks. Their names and reputations were enough for her. And in the same way, every retailer, from the smallest neighborhood grocer to the largest department store or specialty shop, prospered to the degree that his potential clientele trusted his judgment, his sincerity and honesty, and his willingness to be of service.

Where the merchandise came from that was sold in the neighborhood shop or the local A&P, or Wanamaker's or Fields or Macy's, was of practically no interest to the shopper. Most of it carried no name, or merely the name of the shop which sold it. And that was sufficient to satisfy Mrs. Consumer, as it still is, in many instances, today.

What Brand Is It?

But advertising "agents" like Thompson—and perhaps he more than most, because his early success was bound up more intimately than any other agent's with the growth and development of the national magazine—have worked unceasingly to thrust the name of the *manufacturer* into the forefront of the marketing scene, to promote the national brand and the brand name, and thus in a very important sense to make the retailer's name somewhat less important, so that the essential question in many purchases now is not "Where did you buy it?" but "What brand is it?"

The struggle has not been completely resolved, and never will be. Even now, when the dominance of the national brand can scarcely be disputed, the world's largest retailing organization (Sears, Roebuck & Co.) does all but a tiny fraction of its immense volume on "private brand" merchandise, much of it produced by manufacturing subsidiaries or affiliates of Sears, and available only through Sears stores or catalogs.

■ A few other retailers have managed to maintain this position, so enviable from their standpoint. But most have not. Even the giants like A&P, Safeway, Walgreen and the like have had to retreat, step by

Mass movement of grocery goods, including produce, to market was the mark of early grocery chain stores. A&P outlets looked like this in 1927 in New York's Bronx, where the store manager proudly stands by his wares before the day's big rush begins.

step, from their original position as arbiters of the shape, size, smell, taste, composition, character and price of everything they offered for sale in their retail establishments. Retailers are no longer *buyers* for their customers, so much as they are

suppliers of what their customers want. The distinction may sound obscure, but it is of prime importance.

For example: When the battle for dominance between retailer and national brand was at its height, in the decade and a half or so before World War II, retailers for the most part carried national brands reluctantly, and fought their final battle against them across the retail counter, where clerks spent most of their time advising their customers that the store's own private brand merchandise was as good as, or better than, the advertised brand, and usually cost less.

Self Service Changes Everything

For the great bulk of retailers, the battle came to an abrupt end when the retail counter disappeared. Self service changed everything. Retailers welcomed self service because it cut down their sales costs; more business could be done faster, with fewer employes. The retail counter, and the knowledgeable owner or clerk profferring advice behind it, literally disappeared from an amazingly large segment of retailing. The whole character of retailing changed. The customer made her choices, unhindered and unaided, as she passed down aisle after aisle of packaged, labeled, branded merchandise.

Self-service retailing (and later, the concept of the discount store) could not have come about without widely known brands, easily recognizable, with their virtues pre-sold to consumers through advertising. The function of the retail store, and the activity of the customer within it, changed more than most of us realize. Buying decisions, once made with the help of the store personnel across the buying counter, largely are made now before the customer enters the store; a "shopping" expedition is more likely to be an order-filling assignment to satisfy buying decisions already made.

■ The retailer has not given up all his

ability to influence, of course. But the exercise of direct influence, through the retail clerk talking across the counter to the customer, has been shifted to more subtle, less easily noted areas. The family purchasing agent moving down the aisles to fill her predetermined order for goods is constantly assailed by special displays, by beguiling efforts to win impulse purchases from her, and by almost machiavellian attempts, by size, location and attractiveness of display, to shift favorable emphasis from one product or one brand to another.

Retailers' buying decisions, as well as those of their customers, have also shifted in the process. Margins, terms, quality of the goods, etc., are still important, of course. But the retailers' principal concern must now be: "How easily and how quickly will this product move off my shelves, under its own power, with no particular assistance from me? How many of my customers are pre-sold on this product and this brand, or will be presold by the manufacturer's promotion? Will this product, sitting on X square feet of my precious shelves, yield me a better net return per day than some other product occupying that same space?"

Pre-Selling: A Switch to Advertising

Thus, pre-sold national brands, backed with advertising and promotion, made self-service retailing possible in the first place. But self-service retailing in turn strengthens the need for pre-selling and advertising—for products and brands whose virtues are not merely accepted by masses of the public, but are actually sought out by them, so that retailers are almost literally forced to place them on their shelves.

We have been speaking in terms of supermarkets, largely. But pre-selling is also an enormous factor in major purchases, such as appliances and even automobiles. One of the most famous advertising campaigns of all time, mounted for

World War II era saw outdoor and transit ads like these. Today, transit ads are big, carried by 70,000 vehicles in 380 cities.

Chrysler when that manufacturer entered the low-price field with Plymouth, urged buyers to "look at all three." But in actual fact, as innumerable studies have shown, very few new-car buyers shop as many as two makes of cars, and an equally small number shop as many as three dealers. To an amazing extent, they have decided whether they want a Ford or a Chevrolet, a Volvo or a Buick—and which dealer they want to buy it from—before they go into a dealer's establishment.

Media, Not Retailer, Do the Selling

In short, consumer buying decisions have been transferred, in large measure, from the store or the showroom to the pages of newspapers or magazines, or the television screen. Retailing is, more than ever before, order-taking; selling is, more than ever before, advertising.

Retailers advertise, of course; frequently with money supplied to them in the form of advertising allowances by manufacturers whose products they handle. They advertise to induce shoppers to come to their emporium rather than the one across the street; they feature prices and availabilities, and almost half of the

Our recent history benefitted us most

Think for one moment: It would require only 800 people to span the last 50,000 years of man's existence, assuming, of course, that a typical life span is 60 years.

But of those 800 people, 650 would have spent their lives in caves or something less luxurious. Of those 800 people, only the last 70 had any effective means of communicating with one another.

Only six ever saw a printed word. Only four could measure time with any precision. Only the last two used an electric motor. Almost everything that makes up our material world today has been developed during the life span of the 800th person.

—**Sal F. Marino,**
Penton Publishing Co.

country's total advertising is placed by them. They are the principal advertisers in newspapers, and important advertisers in other local media, including radio and television. They use vast quantities of direct mail; they produce sales bulletins and house organs and fashion shows, and

handsome window displays and entertainment for the kiddies. Their advertising is price-and-item advertising, largely designed to develop traffic tomorrow, and it is generally accepted as an essential part of the merchandising scene.

But it is "national advertising"—the promotion of branded merchandise widely available—which spells "advertising" to most people and causes so much discussion in public forums, in academic circles, and in legislative halls.

"National advertising" is the realm of the advertising agency. This is "Madison Ave.," although that largely retail street in New York is not now and never was the home of more than a handful of advertising agencies. This is the world of television and radio commercials, of attractive, colorful magazine and newspaper ads, of painted bulletins and flashing displays, of image-building, of the introduction and exploitation of new and exciting products—of the vigorous promotion of soaps and cigarets, of pain-relievers and instant beautifiers, of automobiles and refrigerators and correspondence lessons in art and, yes, of going to the church of your own choice or contributing to your favorite charity. #

Ten men who shaped the nation's advertising

BY MERLE KINGMAN

James Walter Thompson—a foremost figure in development of advertising and the agency business, made his influence felt largely in the last quarter of the 19th century. He started at 20 as a clerk in 1868 in an agency that he instilled new vigor and new ideas into, bought out and gave his name to ten years later. When Mr. Thompson entered the business, most of it was in religious publications, and it was he who changed the emphasis to the emerging general magazine field, and particularly to women's magazines—and in so doing, contributed importantly to awareness of the woman consumer and efforts of media and advertisers to appeal to and sell to her. A contemporary stated: "It is Thompson, more than any other agent, who has developed the magazine field." In an era of patent-medicine selling and sharp practices, he concentrated on clients with reputable goods and services. By the turn of the century, his agency was pioneering in the type of analysis and planning that marks modern agency service. Mr. Thompson at 69 sold out the agency to his associates in 1916.

F. Wayland Ayer—stamped his imprint on the agency business in many ways, but most of all in his influence on the modern agency commission system, the advertiser-agency-media relationship, and on the service nature of agencies. Mr. Ayer at 20 launched his own agency in 1869, obtaining two kinds of help from his father: Some capital (reputed to be $250) and use of his name for the agency—N. W. Ayer & Son—which the enterprising son hoped would help conceal his youth. Concentrating on newspapers, Ayer soon became the nation's largest agency and remained so for many years. George Rowell, who competed with Mr. Ayer and J. Walter Thompson, wrote in 1906 that Mr. Ayer was "the richest man in this business" and Mr. Thompson "the richest advertising agent in New York." When Mr. Ayer started, agents bought newspaper and magazine space as cheaply as possible and sold it for as much as they could get. Mr. Ayer devised the "open" advertising rate, whereby he told advertisers exactly what he paid for space, provided them media-selection aid and became, in effect, a space buyer rather than space seller.

George P. Rowell——one of the outstanding advertising agents of the 1800s, helped bring stability and facts to space buying and the agency system. Starting as a bill collector for the *Boston Post* in 1858, he became so interested in a New York theater playbill-program carrying advertising that he introduced the idea in Boston. Impressed with his profits, he started his own business as an advertising agent, and by 1871 had amassed a modest fortune ($100,-000). Besides making money in the agency business, he improved it. Originally, the agent collected from the advertiser and paid the publisher, subtracting commissions. If he didn't collect, he didn't pay. Mr. Rowell, cultivating newspaper publishers, established a guarantee of payment by himself as agent—a principle that later became usage. He also preached results of advertising, and means to help foretell them. In 1869, he supplied advertisers for the first time a complete list of 5,411 U.S. newspapers—in *Rowell's American Newspaper Directory.* In it he published circulation figures and under threats of libel suits from outraged publishers, he worked at keeping them honest (he was never sued). He founded *Printers' Ink* in 1888.

Claude C. Hopkins——one of advertising's great copywriters, was associated with Albert Lasker, chairman of Lord & Thomas, for many years in the early 1900s and Mr. Hopkins himself later served as president and chairman of L&T. The two men conceived such famous lines as "the cereal shot from guns" for Quaker Oats Co.'s Puffed Wheat and Puffed Rice. Mr. Hopkins made enough money to retire from Pepsodent toothpaste, a product he nurtured from its beginning. He began his advertising career devising ads for Liquozone germicide, sold via the sampling method, a device he applied to products ranging from tires to patent medicines in later years. He was the first to put coupons in ads offering a free sample. Mr. Hopkins, like John Powers before him, was an advocate of simple, brief copy, commenting: "Brilliant writing has no place in advertising. A unique style takes attention from the subject." His penchant for directness in copy style was based on his intimacy with the Bible, resulting from his leanings toward the ministry in his youth. "I lived and grew to manhood among the poor," he said. "I never tried to write copy for the rich and don't know their reactions. For others, my words will be simple, my sentences short." Mr. Hopkins retired from L&T in 1922 and died ten years later.

Volney B. Palmer—generally is credited with being the first advertising agent, starting in business in the early 1840s and thereby establishing himself as the father of the agency business. His offices were in Boston, New York and Philadelphia. Mr. Palmer commanded a 25% commission from the newspapers for all advertising he placed (plus postage and stationery expenses!), although by the time of his death, probably in the 1850s, others who had entered the agency business were obliged to whittle their commissions down from 25%. Mr. Palmer is described by George P. Rowell, who knew him. ". . . his stout figure, florid countenance, gray hair, bald head, blue coat with brass buttons, gold bowed spectacles, gold headed cane and bandanna handkerchief were known and, to some extent, respected by advertisers and publishers for a considerable term of years."

James H. McGraw—who set out to be a teacher, ended up as a formidable figure in the development of the business paper field and as the creator of the world's largest business paper publishing company. Graduating from a teachers' college, Mr. McGraw sold subscriptions during the summer for the *Journal of Railway Appliances* at $40 a week. After working in various enterprises in business publishing, he joined with John Hill to form McGraw-Hill Book Co. in 1909 (a flip of the coin decided which name came first). Mr. Hill died in 1916. McGraw-Hill Publishing Co. was formed in 1917. McGraw publications were *Electrical World, Electrical Railway Journal, Electrical Merchandising, Engineering Record, Chemical & Metallurgical Engineering* and *The Contractor.* Hill papers were *American Machinist, Power, Engineering & Mining Journal, Coal Age* and *Engineering News. Business Week* was launched in 1929. A foremost part of Mr. McGraw's imprint on business paper publishing was his stress on developing editorial strength as the basis of operations, and he used his teaching talents in long sessions with his editors.

Cyrus H. K. Curtis—founder of Curtis Publishing Co., contributed more to the development of modern magazine advertising than any other one person—and in the doing contributed greatly to the growth of advertising generally. Starting in advertising as a Boston newspaper advertising solicitor, Mr. Curtis, with a partner, launched in 1872 the *People's Ledger* and in 1879 the *Tribune & Farmer,* an agricultural weekly. Neither were startling successes, but Mr. Curtis noticed that a women's feature in the weekly was popular and he made it a monthly supplement. In 1883 he started the *Ladies' Home Journal*, with instant success. Using big "name writers like Louisa May Alcott, he ploughed back money and borrowed heavily for advertising the magazine. In five years he invested a half million in advertising—a huge sum for such a purpose in the 1880s. By 1900, circulation soared to 1,000,000, and advertising led all competition. In 1897, he bought a creaking, old literary weekly, *The Saturday Evening Post*, which, after a slow start, he revitalized with top writers and illustrators. Advertising revenues topped $1,000,000 in 1907; circulation passed 1,000,000 in 1909. *Country Gentleman* was added in 1911. Behind Mr. Curtis' success were vitality, keen understanding of advertising and willingess to invest in it.

John Wanamaker—an innovator in merchandising, advertising and promotion, at 22 opened a men's and boys' store in Philadelphia in 1861 (several days before the firing on Fort Sumter) and invested $24 of his first day's receipts of $24.67 in an ad in the old *Public Ledger*. The ad was a success in attracting customers and from then on Mr. Wanamaker became a heavy and consistent advertiser in good times and bad. In an era when "let the buyer beware" prevailed generally, he was a leader in giving the customer full value. At the same time he shocked traditional retailers with such merchandising stunts as releasing balloons and offering a suit for their return, and with a citywide flood of 100-ft. teaser posters proclaiming "W&B" (for Wanamaker & Brown) preceding follow-up posters with the full story. He ran the first newspaper full page by a store in 1879, and began a schedule of pages in 1888. Other firsts were the first white sale in the U.S. and the first use of electric lighting by a store. He also pioneered home delivery and telephone service. He died in 1922.

John E. Powers——a master copywriter of the late 19th century, was noted for his original use of common sense advertising appeals and simplicity of copy style. Starting as a subscription agent for the *Nation,* he was sent to England in 1868 by Willcox & Gibbs to promote its sewing machines, and he did so with great success, using such novel means as a Drury Lane Theater production, with costumed actors demonstrating the machine as part of the plot, and ads with fast-moving fictional copy telling, "How I won my wife" with the sewing machine. Mr. Powers returned to New York, became publisher of the *Nation,* then joined Lord & Taylor department store to write its ads. Impressed, John Wanamaker hired him away until 1886 when Mr. Powers became a free lance ad counselor, serving then-successful advertisers such as Scott's Emulsion, Beecham's Pills and Macbeth's Lamp Chimneys, reputedly for as much as $100 a day. Stressing copy simplicity, he once said, " 'Fine' writing is not only intellectual, it is offensive "

Albert D. Lasker——who at 26 landed his first agency job at Lord & Thomas in 1898 at $10 a week, became a driving force in advertising—probably the outstanding one of this century in developing national advertising as we know it today. By 1904, he was a general manager (at $52,000 a year) and by the time he dissolved the agency in 1942 he is estimated to have placed three-quarters of a billion dollars of advertising. Although not himself a copywriter, he was an outstanding copy editor and was eminently successful in devising powerful ad themes (with such clients as George Washington Hill of American Tobacco) that sold goods in mass volume. His message was not "come to our store" but, bypassing wholesalers and retailers, he aimed directly at the consumers to build national demand. He preached that advertisers didn't spend enough and in 1912 proposed to clients that they multiply their budgets five to ten times. He offered to finance their advertising with a year's credit; some clients took him on, including Goodyear, Van Camp, and Willys-Overland. Mr. Lasker trained such admen as Benton, Blackett, Hummert, Aveyard, Erwin, Wasey, Getchell, Foote, Cone, Belding and Duane Jones. One chronicler described him as "a driving enthusiast, an inspired salesman, a mesmerist, egotistical, daring, confident and triumphant." He was also a philanthropist and civic leader. He died in 1952.

The way things were in colonial days

In 1775 there were about 2,500,000 people in the 13 colonies. Philadelphia, the largest city, had a population of about 30,000, New York about 22,000. In 1790, one of the first acts of our nation was to take a census. The count: 3,172,000 whites and 600,000 blacks. These numbers did not include Indians nor the many Spanish and French in the Mississippi Valley, the Southwest and Far West. Or the settlers, traders, explorers and adventurers who were beyond the range of the census-takers.

We were a nation of young people. About half the population was under 16. And we were a nation of farmers: 80% of Americans lived off the land. Most of the people were from England and Scotland. At least 10% of the population was Irish. There were 100,000 Dutch, 53,500 French (primarily Huguenots), 21,000 Swedes, 258,000 Germans (including Swiss and Austrians). There were also Sephardic Jews (the first ones came to New York in 1654). Slavs, Italians, Danes, Spaniards and Portuguese were here in smaller numbers.

■ For most people, life was hard but full of opportunity. How well you lived depended, naturally, on where you lived and your social and financial status. In a country without an aristocracy, it was still possible to live like an aristocrat. If you were a tobacco, cotton, rice or indigo planter, you and your family enjoyed a life of leisure. If you lived in the city and had the wherewithal, you had it almost as good. You dined off china, drank your cider from a silver mug, curled your hair, invited your friends to admire your new Oriental rugs, and enjoyed afternoon tea every day.

If you were a craftsman or a small merchant you lived in the back of a store because your house was your store. Your spoons were pewter instead of silver, you ate at a cherry table instead of mahogany, and you wore leather breeches instead of satin. Back on the farm or in the woods,

(This article is adapted from "The Spirit of Seventy Six—1776-1976," copyright, 1974, by the Newspaper Advertising Bureau Inc.)

Colonial dress commonly looked like this. In the backwoods, women carded and wove their own cloth.

where most people lived, it was hand-to-mouth, more difficult the farther you got from cities. Your total cash income might be £2 a year. This came from furs or maple syrup or charcoal. You bartered for most of the things you couldn't produce: Sugar, tea, salt, calico, guns and powder. You ate from a wooden trencher and wore deerskins, waited for the peddler to bring you not only news, but good news.

On the farm and in the woods, women and children were the basic labor force. The wife carded and spun and wove her own cloth. She was the family seamstress and her herbs and simples made her the family doctor. Her chances of dying in childbirth were high, and, because children were extra working hands, she had a large family.

Occasionally, a woman broke through the barriers and was successful in business. The first female traveling salesman was "Mad Anne" Bailey, who had previous careers as a scout and courier on the Indian frontier. Another pioneer business woman was Mrs. Bowling of Petersburg, Va., reputed to own half the town.

Blacks participated in the shaping of our country from the beginning. Crispus Attucks, a black man, was the first to fall during the Boston Massacre. Peter Salem, a former slave, waited until he saw the whites of his eyes and killed a British major at Bunker Hill. Benjamin Banneker of Maryland published six almanacs from 1972 to 1797. Black women rose to prominence, too. Elizabeth Freeman won her freedom in court in the first legal test of the "all men are created equal" concept.

A colonist, in 1776, might live in an elegant Georgian mansion or house, a wattle hut, a New England saltbox or a log cabin. It depended on geography, occupation and wealth.

■ English furniture styles were copied here in walnut, maple and cherry. Cabinetmakers built chests and tables and beds and sold them for less than imports. In the countryside, men were their own carpenters and made their own furniture. All furniture was made to order. You told the cabinetmaker what you wanted, and he created it.

The houses of the rich were elegant. Walls were paneled, floors deep in Oriental rugs. The dining room had tables and sideboards laden with silver candlesticks, ladles, pudding bowls, teapots, tankards, spoons, pitchers, beakers, salt dishes, strainers and porringers.

Beds were usually four-posters with canopies, for privacy and to keep drafts out. There were few corridors; one room led into the next. If you wanted privacy, you popped into your four-poster (with its feather bed) and pulled the curtains around you.

The less affluent lived more simply. A trestle table, a Bible box on a chest or press, rush-seated chairs, a settle (high-backed to keep off drafts), a couple of stools, and that was it. The bald eagle became the national emblem in 1782.

If you were a farmer or settler, your fireplace supplied your heat and most of your light. You could also use rush light (reeds dipped in tallow) or a betty lamp (a saucer filled with oil) or a homemade candle.

Fireplaces were the main source of heat until 1742, when Benjamin Franklin invented the first fuel-conserving device, the Franklin stove. It was basically an iron fireplace pulled away from the wall, so the heat warmed the room instead of going up the chimney. The

Franklin stove cut fuel consumption about 50%.

An iron pot on a crane was the main cooking utensil. A later model of the Franklin stove was designed to hold a pot or kettle on its top. Tables were set with wooden bowls and trenchers, pewter or horn spoons in the country; in more sophisticated homes, salt-glazes, stoneware, imported china and silver knives and spoons (forks weren't much used until the 19th century).

Drinking was from mugs and tankards of pottery, leather bound with metal, wood, pewter or silver—depending on your social and financial status.

Food was stored in casks and baskets. By the time of the Revolution, every rural housewife was a basketweaver. Ash was peeled, weathered and pounded. It was split into thin layers which were soaked in ponds until basketweaving time.

Beautiful quilts were the pride of women and many of their traditional patterns are still cherished today. Curtains, brass andirons, paintings, vases and other decorations were only for rich folk who could afford non-essentials.

What did the colonists drink? Ale, beer, wine, cider, rum from the West Indies, whisky, gin (for the Dutch), rum punch, sillabub (a kind of wine-milk punch), tea, coffee, chocolate and milk. They ate pretty much the same meats we do, and, in wilder areas, fleshed out their menu with deer, rabbit, squirrel, possum, bear or whatever they could shoot or trap. This was supplemented by fish, poultry, beans, puddings, garden produce and orchard fruits. In winter, salt and dried meat and fish were staples and, of course, the only vegetables were those that could be dried or stored in a root cellar.

Workingmen wore leather breeches, aprons, caps, and in the winter, leggings. Skins were plentiful, cheap and durable. Coats were fustian. Farmers usually wore homespun with perhaps a broadcloth coat for Sunday. Settlers wore deerskin and moccasins.

■ As for gentlemen, here's a description of a 1772 dandy: His "hair is loaded with powder and pomatum, the rest of him chiefly consists of French silk, gold lace, fringe, silk stockings, hat and feathers." A typical 1776 outfit was a tailcoat with standup collar and lapels, a waistcoat, ruffled shirt, tight-fitting breeches, knitted wool or silk stockings, silver or brass-buckled shoes, a tricorne hat and a sword. Velvets and satins were favored fabrics, beautifully embroidered. During cold weather, small fur or cloth muffs were worn. Doeskin riding breeches were popular, and Philadelphia breeches had the reputation of being particularly fine.

Until the time of the Revolution, men either curled and powdered their hair (and wore curlers to bed every night) or they wore wigs. Since human hair was hard to get, horse and goat hair were often used. During the Revolution, it became fashionable for men to wear their own hair in a queue tied with a bow. Men carried canes, clutch-style wallets in needlepoint or leather, and snuff boxes. They wore watches, watch fobs, gloves.

Country women wore woolen petticoats

In the colonies, some manufacture was done, but much was imported from mother England and came by sailing ships, taking many weeks.

and an overdress of calico or homespun, worsted stockings and coarse leather shoes. For cold weather, they added a leather jerkin and a woolen cape.

Richly dressed dolls were sent here periodically from London and Paris to show off the newest styles and fabrics. Skirts in 1776 were extremely large, often the hoop was eight yards around. The "in" style was the polonaise, a skirt open in the front to show an underskirt. Ruching, swags, embroidery and ruffles adorned both skirt and underskirt. Waists were small, necklines low, sleeves elbow-length with lace ruffles. Stockings were ribbed, striped or embroidered.

Women's hair was worn very high, extended with pads and little cushions, dressed with pomade or powder, be-ribboned, be-feathered, be-flowered. Stays were straight-laced, very tight and stiff. A characteristic outer garment was a wool cloak, usually red, with a boned hood so it wouldn't mess up a fancy hair-do.

If colonial shoes looked odd it's because there was no difference between left and right. They were both the same. A woman's wardrobe included patch boxes, a case for thimbles and scissors, a pomander box for scent, an oiled linen umbrella, aprons, neckerchiefs, elbow-length gloves, mittens, muffs and folding stick fans. Her jewel box contained brooches, cap pins, rings, bracelets, necklaces, earrings.

Children were dressed like miniature adults. They even wore wigs. Boys wore knee breeches and waist-coats and girls as young as two years old wore stays.

Young ladies were rarely married in white. Their gowns were usually of a delicate hue and were made of costly fabrics, such as brocade, velvet and plush. It wasn't until near the end of the 18th century, when a lace-making machine was invented, that brides began wearing wedding veils. It's reported that the first American bride to wear one was Nellie Curtis, adopted daughter of George Washington.

■ In coffee houses, in clubs, in taverns and inns there was drinking, dining, gossiping, gambling. Whist and Loo were two popular card games. Chess, backgammon and draughts (checkers) had their enthusiasts. So did horse racing, cock-fighting and dicing. Dances were the big social attraction. They usually followed concerts, and the instrumental players supplied the music. They danced minuets, cotillions, Virginia reels. Country folk also danced country dances, reels, jigs and hornpipes, all to the music of the fiddle. They also had quilting bees, husking bees, and big wedding and christening parties.

In the 17th century, the arts were scorned as "useless," but this view subsequently changed. The main theatrical event of 1750 was in New York. A company of comedians (yes, comedians) presented the "'Tragedy of King Richard III,' wrote originally by Shakespeare and altered by Colley Cibber, Esq." In August of 1752, you could have seen "The Merchant of Venice" in Washington. Colonials were music lovers. They played, too—fiddles, cellos, hautboys, French horns, trumpets, drums, flutes, lutes, virginals, spinets, harpsichords, pianos, banjos, guitars, harmonicas, organs, fifes and, out in the country, jew's-harps.

■ Although there was a medical school in Philadelphia, very few people ever saw a trained doctor. Most medicine was do it yourself. In every garden grew herbs and simples such as sassafras, rhubarb, sweet basil, boneset. Or you could visit the apothecary for snakeroot, rutabaga, gum arabic and leeches. Midwives delivered the babies. It wasn't until the late 1700s that any obstetricians were used, and even they they were called "male midwives."

Dentistry hardly existed. You suffered and lost your teeth. False teeth for the gentry were made of bone, wood and metal. Paul Revere, when silversmithing was slow, turned his skilled hand to dentures. Eyeglasses were imported from Germany. You bought them in a general store or from a peddler. They came in five different magnifications, and you merely tried one after another until you could see the pattern of a calico or the lace of a ruffle clearly. Ben Franklin invented bifocals, but not many people used them.

Before 1776, the monetary situation was chaotic. A storekeeper had to cope with three kinds of currency: British, American and Spanish. He would have in his till British coins and paper money of every denomination. He would have American coins and currency. (Although it was prohibited, the first American mint was set up in Massachusetts). Since there was a chronic shortage of small change, people would cut up the Spanish reales: One piece was called one bit, two pieces, two bits. And that's why we call a quarter "two bits."

After 1776, the merchant had to cope not only with pounds, shillings, pence and reales, but the new big copper cents, dismes and half dismes and other American paper money and coinage. Most Americans were suspicious of paper money. Barter was a common way of doing business. A peddler would be paid for a packet of pins in dried fish. He would pay for his lodging at an inn with the fish. The innkeeper would then trade the fish to have his horse shod . . . and so on down the line, until someone ate the fish.

Although the British tried to restrict manufacturing in the colonies, they were, after all, 30 days away by trans-Atlantic boat. So factories flourished here. In 1767, New Jersey alone had eight iron furnaces, 42 forges, one plating mill, one slitting mill, and one steel mill—even though no iron was supposed to be made into goods in the colonies. Elsewhere, there were also grist and saw mills, paper mills, fabric mills, smithies, breweries, cooperages, tanneries, potteries and shipyards (it cost 20% to 50% less to build ships here). Power was water power and people power, although at least one grist mill used horse power.

Most craftsmen had a factory and shop in one, and presided over a journeyman and a few apprentices. Wigmakers, tailors, shoemakers, clockmakers, silversmiths, cabinet makers, bakers, carpenters and blacksmiths settled in every large settlement. You could spot them by their shop signs. Since so many people were illiterate, they used pictures instead of words— a big black boot for a shoemaker, a mortar and pestle for an apothecary, and a striped pole for a barber. Almost everything you

The colonial soldier was without today's helmet and boots.

wore or had in your house was made to order by your neighborhood or traveling craftsman, unless it was imported or you'd made it yourself.

In the winter, when they couldn't farm, farmers and their wives turned their hands to other things. A spinning wheel and loom were standard kitchen equipment. Farmers set up forges in their fireplaces and turned out nails. Others tried their hand at making chairs or butterchurns. If they were skilful, their output soon found a market.

■ Colonial merchants, like merchants today, went where the customers were. The trading post was the suburban store, the peddler the walking catalog. The trading post was the great gathering place where Indians, trappers and settlers brought furs and swapped them for manufactured goods. Many American fortunes started with this fur trade.

Goods sold to Indians were usually priced in beaver skins. Shortly before the Revolution, a trading post in Niagara had a sign with the following price list:

"1 man's shirt . . . 1 beaver or 1 buck

"1 gal. tin kettle . . . 2 bucks

"1 blanket . . . 2 beavers or 3 bucks"

And that's why we still call our money bucks.

Traveling for pleasure was unheard of. Roads were unpaved lanes, dusty in the summer, muddy in spring. They were full of potholes and tree stumps. In the early 1700s it was easier to go from Virginia to London than from Virginia to New York. In 1740 a better network of roads began to develop. The first turnpike was built in 1785, running from Alexandria, Va., to the Shenandoah Valley. The first toll road opened two years later, connecting Baltimore and Yorktown.

■ If you had to travel, you most likely went on horseback. Women rode sideways behind their husbands on pillions (cushions), with a wooden bar to rest their feet on. After 1759, you could take a stage coach from New York to Philadelphia. The trip took three days. Regular stage service opened from Boston to New York in 1765. You rode all day, then stopped at an inn for the night. There were inns about every 15 miles. #

Legendary Helen Resor was tops at JWT.

A copy chief at Compton Advertising, Mary Shomier looks up from work in 1928.

Early women in advertising —all uphill

Peggy "the Hat" King (guess origin of nickname) in 1925 (above) was a copy supervisor in a covey of gifted female talent gathered by Helen Resor at J. Walter Thompson Co.

U.S. women have come a long, long way since Betsy Ross. The advertising business has been no exception to their expanding role, particularly since the '20s. In that decade, however, they had a rough row to hoe, as reported here. On the scene was Taylor Adams, now 86 and retired, copywriter and later account executive in the '20s and '30s at the George Batten Co. (now BBDO), Lord & Thomas (today Foote, Cone & Belding), Young & Rubicam and Arthur Kudner Agency. Here he recalls feminine difficulties and achievements of that era.

BY TAYLOR ADAMS

Women began flowering in the creative departments of agencies in the '20s, but you could hardly have said they were prevalent. With a single outstanding exception, they were either temporary tokenists hired for specific tasks (such as "influencing" decision makers of client or prospect) or more often anonymous footsloggers who rarely made it to title or stockholder. In short, and in the metaphor of a famous headline, a woman in advertising in those days was often a bridesmaid but never a bride.

Evidence of her subordinate status was obvious in a story that persisted in the Chicago office of Lord & Thomas, recalled recently by a retired executive of that agency (who prefers anonymity). He said: "When Pepsodent was brought into the house, a conference was called. Pepsodent's peculiar ability to remove that nasty coating that forms on the teeth was discussed. It was called 'plaque' and all sorts of names. We had a woman in the copy department, quite talented. She worked on everything and was highly regarded. She got all of $4,000 a year. She was at the conference and after the thing had been batted around for a couple of hours, she innocently said: 'You mean, don't you, that Pepsodent removes the film?' Mr. Claude Hopkins, the copy chief, in the next few days, produced the opening campaign and based the whole thing on 'Removes the Film.'" The celebrated copy genius, Mr. Hopkins, in his autobiography, says he was author of the phrase. He was being paid $200,000 a year, according to John Gunther in his book on Albert Lasker, then owner of Lord & Thomas.

Mary's 'Skin You Love to Touch'

The legendary exception to woman's general anonymity was the carefully selected, well trained, well rewarded female crew at J. Walter Thompson Co., under the leadership of Helen Landsdowne Resor, who was rightly called dean of women in advertising in those days. Married to Stanley Resor in 1917, she was brilliant and beautiful. David Ogilvy called her the greatest copywriter of her generation. She coined "The Skin You Love to Touch" for Woodbury Soap, a slogan said to have provoked Albert Lasker, whose agency was then promoting Palmolive with the unexciting "Keep That Schoolgirl Complexion," to exclaim, "Thompson's stolen a march on us! They've put *sex* in soap advertising."

Thompson was the first agency to raise women to major positions and one of the first to elect a woman vice-president— Ruth Waldo, supervisor of women's copy. Around Waldo, Helen Resor assembled a working group of women whose combined talents and specialized capacities have not, I think, been equaled before or since in U.S. advertising.

Peggy 'the Hat' Snares Socialites

In this gallery were Peggy ("The Hat") King; Monica O'Shea, married to famous photographer Nicholas Murai; Blanche Chenery, and two of the gifted Fox sisters, Louise Connell and Janet Wing, both of whom went from JWT into successful careers as magazine editors. There was Mary Beaty, referred to

Daughter of noted adman Albert Lasker, Mary Lasker got ad job against father's wishes. Above: She's an agency vp in 1937.

In pensive mood was Janet Fox, sister of Louise Fox Connell, in a 1925 photograph. A copystar, she became Janet Fox Wing.

In 1930, Anne Hummert was helping hubby Frank Hummert bat out radio spots at Blackett & Sample. They wrote soapers.

Star copywriter at N. W. Ayer, Mabel Hill Souvaine (in 1943 shot) started own agency, then was editor, Woman's Day in '30s.

as Thompson's "walking medical library," and a lady known only by the *nom du travail* of Lucille Platt as she went about gathering the testimonials of socialites, mountain climbers and assorted celebrities who adorned the ads for Pond's, Fleischmann's yeast and Simmons mattresses, products sold by this form of promotion, in which JWT excelled.

Throughout the '20s, women appeared more and more frequently in advertising. Early in the decade, Mabel Hill, a copywriter from N.W. Ayer, started her own agency in New York, in partnership with Harry Winston, sales manager of Wooltex. Later, as Mabel Souvaine, she became editor-in-chief of *Woman's Day*. In 1925, an authentic southern belle, Elizabeth Woody, joined the copy department of the George Batten Co. (later BBDO) when that shop absorbed the Colgate house agency. Woody, some years later, was to become an editor of *McCall's*. Sigurd Larmon, president of Young &

Rubicam, paid high tribute to Louise Taylor Davis as she retired in 1946. Miss Davis had come to Young & Rubicam in 1925 and though never given a title, was generally considered one of the most valuable of the brilliant innovators whose ideas transformed many of the sacred cows of advertising and helped bring the agency, in ten years, up into the Top Three.

The Charleston and Stutz Bearcats

At McCann-Erickson, Dorothy Barstow, assisted by Florence Richards and Margaret Jeesup, created campaigns for Pacific ("Twenty-Mule-Team") Borax and Cheseborough's Vaseline. Barstow married her boss, as did Berta Hendricks at Blackett-Sample in Chicago. Hendricks was credited with inventing "Helen Trent," first of the soap operas. Also in Chicago at the time were Tracy Samuels and Mary Lasker Foreman, both at Lord & Thomas. Mrs. Foreman had forced her way into her father's agency against his violent opposition at a pittance of $8 a week. At Blackman (later Compton Advertising) in New York, Mary Shomier headed a group of women doing campaigns for Ivory soap, Crisco and other brands of Procter & Gamble, then as now, one of the largest advertisers.

Outside the agencies, in retail and manufacturers' promotion, women were finding opportunities and making good. Prominent among these was Bernice Fitzgibbon, who came from Marshall Field to Macy's in New York in 1923. Soon famous for "It's Smart to be Thrifty," she later moved on to Gimbel's where she again hit the bulls-eye with "Nobody, But Nobody Undersells Gimbel's." Fitzgibbon was elected Business Woman of the Year in 1954, and ten years later *Fortune* named her one of the seven top business women in the U.S. At Van Raalte, advertising manager Gay Walton paced the flamboyance of the times, merchandising the rolled-down silk stockings and stepins of John Held's flappers as they swung through the Charleston or hopped out of Stutz Bearcats.

Women in advertising in the Twenties may have been few in number, but they were first rate in quality. They had to be good, to compete in the rough-and-tumble of those years of swift, unregulated growth, before the American Assn. of Advertising Agencies, Assn. of National Advertisers and the Federal Trade Commission brought some semblance of

The well known Fox sisters, both copywriters at Thompson, included Louise Fox Connell —her usual glamorous self in this 1927 shot taken on vacation in Guaymas, Mexico.

law and order to a business headed for multi-billion-dollar volume. Some of them had talent that transcended the demands of their advertising jobs and took them into other, more prestigious fields. Such a one had come to George Batten Co.

in 1923 to write copy for the American Greeting Card Assn. She soon left, and years later, passing Brentano's, I saw her face on the jacket of the best-selling novel, "Gentleman's Agreement" by Laura Hobson. #

Saga of N.W. Ayer, oldest U.S. agency

Ulysses Grant was in the White House. Jay Gould and James Fisk were cornering the gold market in a series of shenanigans that would lead to the financial panic of Black Friday. Rails had just linked both oceans, and carpetbaggers were still running rampant in a defeated South.

That was the year 1869, the year Francis Wayland Ayer—native of Massachusetts, schoolmaster at the age of 15, college dropout (the University of Rochester, because of family economics), space salesman for religious newspapers—went into business for himself as an advertising agent 107 years ago this month, in Philadelphia.

At the age of 21, as the story goes, he felt that advertisers might resent doing business with so young a man. So he named his company for his father, Nathan Wheeler Ayer, and put himself anonymously after the ampersand in "N. W. Ayer & Son." He also put all his savings, $250, into capitalizing the new business.

■ He gave it all his energies. A few years later, exhausted in the middle of a night's work at the office, he scrawled on his desk pad the phrase, "Keeping Everlastingly At It." In the morning, Mr. Ayer's first partner, George Wallace, saw the notation and added two words to complete what became the motto of America's oldest advertising agency: "Keeping Everlastingly At It Brings Success."

Everlastingly at it the agency has been since. Successful, too. At times through its history, Ayer has been the largest U. S. advertising agency. At times, it has slipped, but not, since the early formative years, below the top 20 agencies in America.

'I'll Never Be Satisfied Again'

An the six chief executives (the latest elected last month) who have guided the agency since its founding have shared an appreciation of profit and diligence and the ability to build the business in most all of the years since 1869. The agency needed to learn the lesson of keeping everlastingly at it only once. "The biggest mistake I ever made," Wayland Ayer once told B. C. Forbes, the publisher, was

made in "the first year we did $1,000,000 of business. We thanked the Lord, and that is about all we did. The boat drifted with all hands resting on the oars. The next year we did less than $800,000.

"I then vowed that if I were forgiven for having been satisfied, I never would be satisfied again so long as I lived."

The Ayer agency, with all its years in business and so many of them in conservative Philadelphia until headquarters moved to New York three years ago, does have a "traditional" reputation. But a look at Ayer past and present shows that one

significant tradition has always been to establish standards of excellence and not be satisfied unless they are exceeded.

That's one tradition. Integrity is another. So is innovation.

Ayer Launches Open Contract

The Christian ethic guided Wayland Ayer in everything he did. A devout Baptist and at one time president of the Northern Baptist Convention, Mr. Ayer brought an element of morality to the rough-and-tumble, often cutthroat advertising agency business.

Six chief executives of N W Ayer

Francis W. Ayer
1869-1923

Wilfred W. Fry
1923-1936

H. A. Batten
1936-1958

Warner Shelly
1958-1966

Neal W. O'Connor
1966-1976

Louis Hagopian
1976-

Ayer's wasn't the first American advertising agency. That distinction is usually accorded to another Philadelphian, Volney B. Palmer, who in the 1840s was selling space in newspapers in Pennsylvania and New Jersey and receiving commissions from the publishers. He had a lot of competition even before Wayland Ayer came along.

But Mr. Ayer made an early decision that changed the nature and course of the agency business. His first major innovation was the development of the "open contract" between advertiser and agency. During the first six years, Ayer & Son operated pretty much like any other advertising agent, representing publications (in Mr. Ayer's case his first were 13 religious weeklies) and selling space in them to advertisers. In 1876, Mr. Ayer took the bold step that changed the nature of the agency business and also made it a more principled one. He decided to represent the advertiser—the advertiser *alone*—in dealing with media.

From this decision developed the first Ayer open contract, whereby the agency became the exclusive representative of the advertiser, purchasing media on his behalf and being compensated by the advertiser on the basis of a percentage of what the advertiser paid for space. The open contract was truly that: the agency's books were open to the client, and the function of the agency was to represent the best interests of the advertiser; to consider his needs first, to spend his money wisely, and to be concerned with how he presented and marketed his products.

An anecdote told by Wayland Ayer reveals the sense of principle that led him to set higher standards for the agency business:

"The gentleman who had succeeded to the editorial chair in the office of the paper which first gave me employment in Philadelphia came to me in the latter part of 1874 with the remark that he would like to have a serious talk with me about my business future. 'I have come to think a good deal of you, personally,' he said, 'and I have high regard for your ability; but I wish you were in a business I could respect as much as I respect you.'

Ad Agent 'Nothing but Drummer'

"Looking me straight in the eye, he added: 'What is an advertising agent, anyway? Nothing but a drummer—and he never will be anything else. No one has any respect for him!' Then said he, 'I believe I am in a position to arrange for you a connection with an organization of the highest standing, and I also believe you will be a credit to the concern.'

"His sweeping condemnation of advertising agents both hurt and challenged me.

BUSINESS RULES
— OF —
AYER & SON'S ADVERTISING AGENCY,
PHILADELPHIA.

I.—The offices shall be ready for *business occupancy* by 7.55 A. M. every day.

II.—All employees, unless absent from the city, or specially excused by one of the firm, are expected to be at their respective desks ready for business at 8 o'clock sharp.

III.—Three quarters of an hour, between 12 M. and 2 P. M., will be allowed each person for lunch, which must in every case be completed by the last-named hour. Such arrangement must also be made as will always insure the presence of one or more representatives of each department during these hours.

IV.—During business hours, loud talking, jesting, laughing, or smoking will not be allowed, and the employees are particularly requested to avoid conversation with each other, or with those not connected with the office, about any matters other than those strictly pertaining to the business of the firm.

V.—Each employee will occupy his own desk, which will be supplied with all necessary appliances; and his intercourse with any other employee during business hours must be as infrequent and of as short duration as the exigencies of the case will permit. Letters or papers concern those only in whose possession or on whose desk they may be.

VI.—Our business is divided into *four distinct departments*, each under the charge of a chief clerk, to whom all assistants in that department will look for their instructions, and who in turn will account to the firm for all that transpires in his department.

VII.—It is preferred that so far as practicable all communications between the different departments should be through their respective heads, rather than between the assistants.

VIII.—An office-boy will at all times be in attendance for the delivery of any messages that may be required in the course of business between the various departments. All such messages not delivered in person must be sent by the boy; and loud calling from one desk or department to another is *strictly prohibited*. The office-boy must never be sent outside of the building, unless by one of the firm.

IX.—The hours of business will be from 8 A. M. to 6 P. M., unless otherwise specified; but each day's business *must be completed*, so far as practicable, *that day*, even if to do so requires extra work. Preparations for departure should not begin before 6 o'clock. Any person desiring to leave earlier should obtain permission from the head of his department, or from the firm.

X.—All persons connected with this agency are requested to wipe their feet before entering, to cultivate neatness in personal appearance, to keep their desks clean and tidy, externally and internally, and especially to avoid loitering about the halls or entrance. REMEMBER! ours is a business place; we mean business; and we desire all our employees to look and act business.

XI.—All salaries will be paid every Saturday afternoon; and the cashier is forbidden to advance any money during the week on salary account, except on presentation of a written order signed by one of the firm.

XII.—The books of account and the newspaper files are the property of the firm, and the only persons having any right of access to either are those to whom their care has been particularly entrusted. Other employees desiring information from either must obtain it from these persons, or under their direction. Under no circumstances will any employee be allowed to remove from the office any papers belonging to the files, except it be for business purposes; and then they must be obtained from the chief clerk of the Registry Department, and to him returned.

XIII.—All private communications addressed to employees will be deposited in a box set apart for that purpose, to which all can have access at the close of each business session, i. e., at noon and at night; but the perusal or answering of any personal letter during business hours is strictly prohibited.

Having always endeavored to render each position in our gift as agreeable as possible to its incumbent, we in return expect from every employee a careful attention to our interests, and a ready compliance with all our requests. We shall therefore anticipate from all such a careful observation of these rules as will make them mutually beneficial. Should they at any time be found unjust or onerous in any particular case, it will afford us pleasure, on satisfactory evidence, to at once remedy such defect.

April 2, 1877.   *N. W. Ayer and Son*

N. B.—Regulations for the management of the different Departments can be obtained from their respective Heads.

If you think today's management is a little fussy about tardiness and those long lunch hours, read this 1877 Ayer office bulletin. Feel better?

Restraining my feeling, however, I asked to be allowed to think the matter over until the next day. My reply then was something like this:

"'The proposition you made does not appeal to me. I have put my hand to this plow and, by the help of the Lord, I am going to finish the furrow; and before I have finished it, if we both live, you are coming to me some day to say that you respect me for my business as well as for myself'."

■ Mr. Ayer took his open-contract idea to the head of Dingee & Conard, a rose grower to whom he had been selling advertising, and agreement was reached that Ayer & Son would be exclusive agent to buy advertising, that the client would know, but keep confidential, all the prices that the agency paid for space, and that the agency would be paid 10% of the net cost of the space. This rate of commission, which proved unprofitable, was raised to 12½% after a year. Shortly after 1878, the rate was stabilized at 15%, but Dingee & Conard, a comparatively small account in later years, was kept on at 12.5%.

Mr. Ayer's development of the open contract, though greeted with disdain and some dismay by his competitors, had an immediate effect on the advertising business.

Some agents adopted the Ayer system of representing the advertiser; among those were several of today's leading agencies or their successors. Others went in the opposite direction and henceforth were known as publishers' representatives, another important force in advertising today. The lines of distinction were clear: No longer (at least until the contemporary phenomenon of the media-buying service) was one agency to be engaged in both buying and selling space.

Mr. Ayer had made the agency business more moral, and it started making him more money. And as it grew, Ayer & Son needed managerial help. While the founder had the talents and instincts of an entrepreneur, as well as a somewhat demanding coolness in dealing with people (said President William Howard Taft of Mr. Ayer: "When he wants a thing he gets it, and he doesn't mince matters about getting it, either"), new managers and partners added new dimensions and expertise to the agency.

Henry N. McKinney lacked Ayer's financial acumen; he had led three publishing companies downhill in the six years before Ayer took him on as a clerk in 1875 at $15 a week. But he had a drive and ebullience that made him an exceptional exponent of Mr. Ayer's idea of agency acting on behalf of the advertiser. He became the salesman for the agency.

Clients: Wanamaker, Harvard

In its first dozen or so years, Ayer & Son

STEINWAY
THE INSTRUMENT OF THE IMMORTALS

THE KING'S HENCHMAN, *painted for the* STEINWAY COLLECTION *by* N. C. WYETH

Prices: $875 *and up*

When Raymond Rubicam worked for Ayer in 1919, he did the famous "immortals" slogan. Artist: N. C. Wyeth.

placed any kind of advertising it could get—legal notices, help wanted, lost dogs. It advertised Kennedy's Ivory Tooth Cement, which made "Everyone His Own Dentist," and "Rock & Rye, a Sure Cure for Lung Diseases. $4 per Gal."

But other more enduring names appeared on the agency's ledgers almost from the beginning: John Wanamaker,

Kick-off teaser campaign

Ayer's Camel ad at left was a teaser followed by the ad below when the brand was introduced in 1915.

Tomorrow there'll be more CAMELS in this town than in all Asia and Africa combined!

CAMEL
CIGARETTES
Are Here!

To Cigarette Smokers of America

Camels have arrived! Here is a cigarette made of *blended* choice Turkish and choice Domestic tobaccos that produces a finer flavor, a better fragrance, than either kind of tobacco smoked straight!

Camel Cigarettes *will not* sting the tongue and *will not* parch the throat. They *do not* leave any unpleasant cigaretty after-taste.

Compare Camels for quality, for flavor, with any cigarette in the world! *And make your comparison today!*

Please note that Camel packages contain neither coupons nor premiums. Smokers do not look for them, because they realize that the cost of the tobaccos prohibits their use.

Camel Cigarettes sell 20 for 10c

R. J. REYNOLDS TOBACCO CO., Winston-Salem, N. C.

35

whose fame was spreading far beyond Philadelphia, was an early customer. Montgomery Ward & Co., born of the Granger movement, advertised its mail order business in the Ayer religious lists. Ads were placed for Whitman's chocolates, Ferry seeds, Singer sewing machines, Lippincott books and, in the significant category of educational institutions, correspondence courses in telegraphy and Harvard College.

Armed with the Ayer contract, Mr. McKinney became the new business man *extraordinaire* in the agency's first half century.

On a new business call in 1897, Mr. McKinney set the stage for another Ayer first: The first market research study undertaken by an advertising agency. He wanted the Nichols-Shepard threshing machine account in Battle Creek, Mich., then a client of the rival George P. Rowell agency. The prospective client refused to let Mr. McKinney see the list of papers in which he advertised, telling him to find out for himself where to sell threshing machines.

Back to Philadelphia, and the agency sent telegrams to agricultural officials of every state and to publishers who knew about harvesting conditions. When the information came in, it was compiled to show the production of grains by states and counties. The agency also analyzed the circulations and advertising rates of newspapers that reached farmers in each of the districts. Within four days of his first meeting, Mr. McKinney was back in Battle Creek. He got the account, one with an $18,000 budget.

Mr. McKinney was largely responsible for getting the agency involved in the "creative" side of the business. Wayland Ayer had long held that agencies should not write ads, insisting that clients knew more about their products than the agency did. But advertisers were realizing that what was said about them was becoming as important as where and how often. In 1888, the agency hired Jarvis A. Wood, "a young man with a gift of ready words," to devote part of his time to writing ads

Ten oldest agencies— which is oldest?

N. W. Ayer & Son, started in 1869, took over Coe, Wetherill & Co. in 1877, and that gave Ayer the basis for the claim to be oldest agency in the U. S. Coe, Wetherill, it seems, succeeded Joy, Coe & Co., which bought out Volney B. Palmer's agency, which was started in 1841. Thus, Ayer today is either 107 years old or 135 years old. The J. Walter Thompson Co. has been known as such since 1878, when James Walter Thompson bought out Carlton & Smith, which opened in 1864. So JWT is either 99 or 112.

Thus, America's oldest advertising agencies are Ayer, started in 1869 or 1841, depending on how you count; Thompson, begun in 1864 or 1878; Albert Frank-Guenther Law, begun in 1872; Cramer-Krasselt, 1900; D'Arcy-MacManus, 1906; Campbell-Ewald, 1911; Griswold-Eshleman, 1912; Erwin Wasey and Doe Anderson, 1915; and Edwin Bird Wilson, 1916. #

for the agency's customers. In 1892, Ayer was the first agency to hire a full-time copywriter. By 1900—the year when Ayer employes first got Saturday afternoon off (just in the summer)—a separate copy department was established.

■ Other changes occurred in the last decades of the 19th century. In 1880, billings were $367,000. By 1889, they increased to $2,030,000 (with profits of $58,000). As early as 1882, N.W. Ayer claimed to be the largest U. S. agency. The roster of employes rose from 40 in 1880 to 160 at the turn of the century. The agency issued its "American Newspaper Annual," now the yearly "Ayer Directory of Publications."

The agency, which had maintained a policy of dealing with newspapers exclusively, followed the lead of Commodore J. Walter Thompson and moved into advertising in magazines. Magazines and, specifically Curtis Publishing Co., Ayer's Philadelphia neighbor, are a significant part of the story of N W Ayer.

Never Underestimate Power of . . .

Edward Bok, in his life of Cyrus H. K. Curtis, reported on the publisher's difficulties with the early growing pains of the *Ladies' Home Journal.* Mr. Curtis told Wayland Ayer of his plans to double the size and the subscription price of the magazine and that he planned a $200,000 advertising campaign, through Ayer, to announce the changes. But he had to have that amount of credit. Mr. Ayer's reply was, "That doesn't scare me," and he

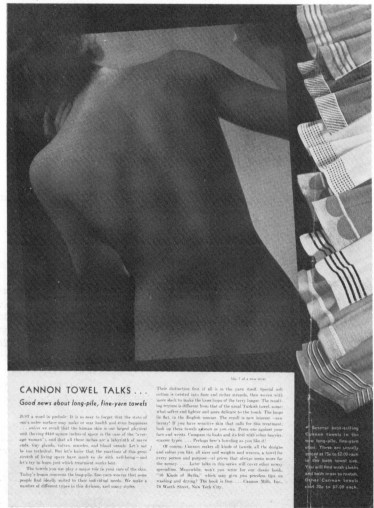

First advertising with nude was a 1933 Cannon Towel ad, with color photograph by Edward Steichen. Cannon has been an Ayer client since 1920.

also guaranteed another $100,000 in notes which Mr. Curtis obtained from his printing paper supplier.

Today, many of the agency's 400,000 advertisements that comprise the "Ayer Collection of Business Americana" in the Smithsonian Institution are pages from *The Saturday Evening Post,* and the old Curtis Bldg. and the old Ayer Bldg. look diagonally at each other across Washington Square. The agency's headline "Never Underestimate the Power of a Woman," has been etched on the minds of two generations of media buyers.

But back at the turn of the century, the triumph of Henry McKinney's advertising career came with the winning of the National Biscuit Co. account and the marketing success that Ayer helped create for a product the agency named Uneeda Biscuit. The product was one of the first to feature a staple food ready for use and sold in a distinctive and airtight package. National Biscuit budgeted an unprecedented $1,000,000 for first-year advertising, an intricately planned campaign, and in 1900 the old-time cracker barrel was doomed as modern packaging and mass marketing arrived.

The new century opened with Ayer in a solid position of leadership, continuing to innovate, continuing its traditional demand for excellence. The business-getting department had its efforts buttressed by national advertising that Ayer directed for itself at business leadership in newspapers, magazines and the advertising trade press. Many advertising people today recall the regularity with which Ayer advertisements appeared from 1909 to 1957 on the covers of *Printers' Ink,* a magazine ironically that once was owned by the rival George Rowell agency.

Large companies paid more attention to advertising and they paid more to Ayer. New accounts came in: American Tobacco, H. J. Heinz, Cluett Peabody, American Sugar Refining, International Silver, Cadillac, Steinway. The agency developed institutional campaigns to develop favorable attitudes toward the American Telephone & Telegraph Co. and Western Union.

The agency moved twice to larger quarters, and opened branches in New York, Boston, Chicago, Cleveland before World War I. But by then Messrs. Ayer and McKinney, the latter in poor health, were aging. And for Wayland Ayer, the attractions of his extensive dairy farming interests in upstate New York were powerful pulls, as well as a fresh challenge to his entrepreneurial spirit: Step by step, he had acquired farm land, bred strong Jersey stock and taken over the marketing for other farmers. The butter produced by and for his Meridale Farms commanded a premium from hotels in

Ford was an Ayer client in 1927 with this ad for a sporty model at $495. Five other models in the newspaper ad ranged down in price to $385.

New York, Philadelphia and Atlantic City.

Other agencies now were growing faster than Ayer. The company had no individual coming up through the ranks who could grasp and manage the whole business. Ayer turned outside and hired, in succession, two managers. But, following two thorough shake-ups, the two outsiders again were outside. From that time on, Ayer grew its own top executives.

The man who was finally tapped for the job of managing the agency was family. Wilfred W. Fry had married Mr. Ayer's oldest daughter in 1904. He was a YMCA worker, and not until 1909 did he accept his father-in-law's invitation to join the agency. In 1911 he became a partner. Mr. Ayer felt that he was ready to become manager in 1916.

Wilfred Fry guided Ayer for 20 years, tumultuous years of war, boom, depression and recovery. Like his father-in-law, Mr. Fry was regarded as a highly-principled, dignified business executive, a paternalistic individual, sound with a dollar—and,

employes recalled, somewhat reluctant to part with it.

Peacetime 1919: Billings Double

Advertising became an instrument for social action in World War I, and Ayer contributed advertising for the first three Liberty Loan drives. With peacetime, advertising began to boom; Ayer's billings more than doubled from $6,500,000 to $13,700,000 in one year, 1919. New partners came into the agency. At the time of Wayland Ayer's death in 1923, there were five young Turks, all with a dozen years in the agency, all representing the business management or account side of the agency.

They were good at new business. William Armistead got from R. J. Reynolds the assignment to introduce Camel cigarets. The Canada Dry account was won by J. M. Mathes (who, like many other Ayer alumni—Messrs. Young, Rubicam, Marschalk, Lewis, Gilman—later saw his name on the door of another agency). These achievements are chronicled in the

600-page volume on Ayer, "The History of an Advertising Agency," that Ralph M. Hower wrote and the Harvard University Press published in 1949. But credits to the copywriter(s) who came up with "I'd Walk a Mile for a Camel" and "Down from Canada Came Tales of a Wonderful Beverage" are not recorded there.

Ayer benefited in the boom years. By 1930, its billings of $38,000,000 were three times higher than they had been in any year of Wayland Ayer's lifetime. The agency maintained its staid shibboleths: No paid-for testimonials from film stars, society matrons or heroes of the hour; no emphasis on bad breath or body odor; and, in a policy that cost them Mathes and Canada Dry at the time of Repeal, no liquor accounts.

But the tradition of innovation was at work, too. Ayer in 1919 became the first advertising agency to establish a public relations department. And it became the pioneering agency, so far as radio was concerned, as it later would be with television.

Eddie Cantor, Gershwin in Radio

In 1922, Ayer broadcast the first radio commercial, for Shuron Optical, over KDKA, Pittsburgh. The next year came the first sponsored series of radio entertainment, "The Eveready Hour" of music,

What's in a name?

Ayer's Henry N. McKinney brought in the National Biscuit (Nabisco) account in 1898, and it was he who named it the Uneeda biscuit—a name subsequently described as containing 13 letters and worth at least $1,000,000 a letter and also as the best known trademark in the world.

lectures, dramatic sketches and humor, for the National Carbon Co. Two years later, AT&T, aided by its agency, made it possible for programs to reach a number of stations simultaneously, and the "Eveready Hour" became the first network radio show. Other firsts with the medium included the first adaptation of a novel ("Show Boat") for commercial radio, and the introduction of Eddie Cantor and George Gershwin to radio audiences.

When the Ford Motor Co. became an account in 1927, Ayer began expansion overseas, opening offices in Europe and Latin America. The agency kept its presence there during the 1930s, but returned home with World War II and—among the major U.S. agencies—was late going back.

Creatively, Ayer was doing very visible and attractive ads in print. In connection with its advertising for Steinway, De Beers, Container Corp., the French Line and other accounts, the agency was commissioning original work from such artists as Rockwell Kent, N. C. Wyeth, Covar-

The Story of a Ladder.

Once upon a time, so the story goes, a ladder drifted upon the shore of a distant island—most likely one that is now ours. In doubt as to its intended use the natives began to "pow-wow" about it. This ended in the formation of two parties; one contending that the rungs were made to hold the sides together, and the other that the sides were made to hold the rungs apart. So the matter rested. After a time a sailor came to the island and, seeing the ladder, promptly put it up against a tree and gathered some fruit he wanted. Something quite like this often happens in the world of business. Many men talk about Newspaper and Magazine Advertising—but do not try it. Finally another comes along and applies it to its intended use of securing trade.

Is this your case? Is there any trade you desire? Shall we show you what we know about the advertising ladder? Is this your year? It's January now you know.

Newspaper Advertising
Magazine Advertising

N. W. AYER & SON, Philadelphia.

A house ad for N. W. Ayer running in Harper's in 1898 used a parable to make its selling point.

rubias, Picasso, Dufy, James Thurber. A Cannon Mills ad was the first to use a color photograph, and Edward Steichen shot the picture.

The Depression hit all advertising agencies hard. And, along with fewer and smaller budgets and more aggressive competition to get them, came a new wave of skepticism about advertising. Books like "100,000,000 Guinea Pigs" and "Skin Deep" cited instances of advertising deception, and with the New Deal, the consumer found a sympathetic ear for his grievances in Washington. Former President Taft had attended the 50th anniversary banquet for the Ayer agency in 1919. There is no record that Franklin Roosevelt took any notice of the diamond anniversary in 1941, though an Ayer art director, Charles T. Coiner, had supplied the design for the National Recovery Administration's Blue Eagle some years before.

Ayer was slower in recovering from the Depression and lost ground to competitors during the final years of Mr. Fry's regime. His idealism and integrity could not alone cope with the rapid pace of change in advertising. And internecine power struggles among management following Mr. Fry's death in 1936 shook the limestone walls of the House of Ayer, the 14-story building near Independence Square that the agency had put up in 1929.

Through the summer and fall of 1936, meetings and litigations ensued over who had the right to purchase Mr. Fry's widow's stock and assume control of the agency. George H. Thornley, one of four directors of the Ayer Corp., lost in a bid for control. It was a period of bitterness, airings of some passion, and the fight was liberally covered in the press. But when the limestone chips were swept away,

Ayer had a new president. Harry A. Batten, at 39 (the same age as Ayer's current chairman, Neal W. O'Connor, when he assumed the presidency), had come up through the ranks and been head of the copy department for seven years. He knew every phase of advertising. Mr. Batten could be tough, but he cared about the copywriters and the art directors, not just the counting room.

Morale rose, but business sagged in the wake of dissensions that had plagued Ayer. It wasn't until 1942 that the agency began to recover volume continuously. Although Ayer had pioneered in radio advertising, its radio department had not kept up with developments, partly because Mr. Fry personally disliked radio advertising. And much of advertising's growth in the pre-World War II years was in radio.

Mr. Batten and his associates took time, but they took hold. By 1941, Ayer's share of national advertising dollars was rising again. And in 1942, the agency was again paying dividends on its stock after a four-year hiatus.

■ World War II brought a new set of situations. For one thing, Ayer management decided against taking on free-spending "war baby" accounts, unless they offered post-war potential as peacetime clients. Mr. Batten could see the future for civil air transport, and Ayer's sole major new defense supplier client was Boeing Aircraft Co., unless one counts the U. S. Army. In 1940, Ayer won the Army recruiting account for the first time.

Dancing Cigarets Come to Tv

In the 1940s, the agency's rejuvenated radio department broadened its pioneering role to that new medium, television. It began telecasting University of Pennsylvania football games (for Atlantic Refining) in 1941 when the Federal Communications Commission first permitted commercial sponsorship of tv shows. This was strictly experimental; the first broadcasts reached 150 tv sets.

By 1946, Ayer produced the first commercial telecast program (for AT&T) and specials for many other clients. They were soon into sustained network programs, like the Sealtest Big Top, and *Variety's* 1948 award for the best commercial on

But Cecil hated coffee

One of the alltime great copywriters was George Cecil, who hated coffee, although Ayer had a big coffee account. In the 1920s and 1930s, Cecil wrote much of the agency's coffee copy. As a matter of fact, it was Cecil who invented the phrase "coffee break."

Far up in the North where the gold is mined they call for "Canada Dry"

CANADA DRY

Canada Dry ad by Ayer ran in 1926.

television went for a line of Lucky Strikes that popped out of a pack and danced across the screen in a commercial that Ayer produced for $6,800.

Through the 1950s and into the 1960s under Mr. Batten and then Warner S. Shelly, who became president in 1951 and chief executive in 1957, Ayer continued to progress steadily, but at a pace more sedate than some of the new gung-ho creative agencies that joined Ayer in the Top Ten and, on occasion, nudged it down a peg or two.

Ayer continued to set and meet high standards and to innovate. It began applying the computer to marketing and media analysis. When one client, Breck, wanted to sell in the East, and another, Hills Bros. coffee, sought a western audience, Ayer people went to publishers with the new idea of split-run advertising. *The Saturday Evening Post* and *Life* turned them down, but *Look* was hungry, and the concept of regional editions was born. Ayer then began the practice of regional buys on network television.

Did Ayer Need 'Fire in Belly?'

The agency, which in all likelihood has won more awards than any other (and which for years gave out one of its own, the Ayer Cup for excellence in newspaper typography), continued to win a good share. Ayer could be termed both an account man's and a creative man's agency. Critics said there could have been a little more fire in the belly but it certainly was also a gentleman's agency.

N. W. Ayer was a respecter of people. "No business," Mr. Batten wrote, "can be better than the people in it. We believe in getting and keeping the most gifted people we can find. We also believe that, once having got them, we must do everything possible to develop them to the fullest extent of their potentialities."

Mr. Batten further cemented Ayer to Philadelphia. He led in the rehabilitation of Society Hill and the development of a food distribution center. His public service extended to space: He became the volunteer financial advisor to the astronauts, negotiating to obtain insurance for them and for the sale of their stories. He died in 1966 at a civic meeting, leaving a profound impact on his city and on advertising. When *Time* had run a lead article on advertising, "The Visible Persuaders," the editors had put Harry Batten's picture on the cover.

Warner Shelly had joined Ayer's business department, at $17 a week, in 1923, the year the founder died. He came up through the account side, and under his leadership, the agency, attaining the $100,-000,000 mark in billings, made major contributions to the marketing success of such clients as De Beers, the Bell System, Plymouth, United Air Lines, Du Pont, Carrier and Cannon Mills.

Never Underestimate the Power of a Woman!

JOURNAL

Dating back to 1950, Ayer's ad for the Ladies' Home Journal included its now famous slogan.

An 'Excited Leprechaun'

As *Printers' Ink* pointed out, "Shelly of N. W. Ayer: How he runs the house built to last forever . . . He takes pride in the way Ayer's operation is planned not for the big new account that may come in, not for a meteoric rise in billings next year, but for a stable growth and, above all, permanence. Shelly looks like an excited leprechaun when he talks about Ayer as the agency that will last forever, That's the way a business should be planned, he feels. And, as he often declares, with the implication that others tend to lose sight of the fact: 'An agency is a business'."

Neal W. O'Connor, Ayer's fifth chief executive, was elected president in 1965 and, on Mr. Shelly's retirement, became

A DIAMOND IS FOREVER

A 1958 magazine ad promoted De-Beers diamonds, a loyal Ayer account since 1939.

chairman in 1973. He, too, continued the tradition of growing up in the agency, having come up through account management. And it's a tradition of which he approves.

"All other things being equal or nearly equal," he has said, "I'm in favor of a management that knows its company intimately—its history, its traditions, its philosophy, most of all, its skeletons."

But in today's business climate of earlier retirements and second careers, Mr. O'onnor did not plan to be running Ayer as long as some of his predecessors did. He has been a little more in a hurry. And the pace of change—planned change—has stepped up at Ayer.

■ The agency has had its downs, but mostly ups, in the past decade. A real blow was the loss of the $28,000,000 Plymouth account in 1966, the largest account move to that time in advertising history. The agency entered 1967 billing at the rate of only $88,000,000.

But in the period since, the agency's business has more than doubled, to $200,-000,000 in 1975. Of the top 20 agencies, only two have grown at a faster rate than Ayer in the past ten years.

New business has come from such places as John Deere, Economics Laboratory, Helene Curtis, Nestlé, Scholl, Kraftco, Olympia Beer, Goodyear, General Motors, Sunbeam, DuPont and the U.S. Army Recruiting Command.

Adversity, in some cases, has been turned to triumph. In 1967, there were problems with the AT&T account that threatened a client relationship dating back to 1908. But the new, young managers and creative people at Ayer kept the business with a presentation so exciting that the Bell System took space in ADVERTISING AGE to congratulate the agency, under the headline, "Never underestimate the power of a nonagenarian."

The agency has acquired full-service agencies in Los Angeles and Seattle and merged another into its Chicago office.

■ And Ayer has gone international again, through Ayer Barker Hegemann International BV, a partnership with leading British and German agencies that is now represented in Canada, the Netherlands, Belgium, Italy and Switzerland, and has its eyes on the remainder of Europe and on the Far East, too.

With the move toward world-wide growth and to make the agency more a business than a personal institution, N. W. Ayer & Son even changed its name, to N W Ayer ABH International. A stroke of the pen erased the founder from the firm.

Mr. O'Connor and his colleagues in top management, the then vice-chairman Louis T. Hagopian and president Robert P. Zabel, added new resources to strengthen service to clients and attract new customers to the place still referred to as the House of Ayer. A marketing services group has developed or contributed to the success of dozens of new consumer products. An expanded Ayer public relations services division is one of the largest in any agency, and Ayer's agency-within-an-agency, Creative/Contact, has assumed recognized leadership in industrial and business advertising.

Some of the traditions have fallen at a more aggressive Ayer. The agency pioneered in advertising in the feminine hygiene product category and has been in (and out of) the liquor business.

■ The fact that the agency reports its billings is in itself an innovation; for a century money was a very private matter.

Wayland Ayer and three of his successors set themselves apart from the advertising agency industry in another way. Ayer was the holdout that refused to join the American Assn. of Advertising Agencies. Today, Ayer is not only in the Four A's, but Mr. O'Connor was its 1975 chairman.

In 1973, the agency consolidated its two largest offices by moving Philadelphia operations to New York. Ayer now occupies three floors at 1345 Sixth Ave. Early this year, the Ayer Bldg. in Philadelphia was sold.

As of March 25, Ayer is operating under the leadership of its sixth chief executive in 107 years. On Mr. O'Connor's recommendation and in what he described as "a move from strength in the succession process," the board of directors elected Mr. Hagopian chairman. A veteran of 12 years in the automotive industry, Lou Hagopian joined Ayer 16 years ago. Mr. O'Connor remains active in the business in the new position of chairman of the executive committee.

It's a lean, swift and flexible agency now, probably more so than in the past. But the traditions of demanding excellence, of integrity and innovation are there. And Ayer people expect to continue to be keeping at it . . . everlastingly. #

Launching Bicentennial with 'USA Inc.' marketing plan

In this Bicentennial period, it is appropriate to examine the underlying cause of our economic problems, rather than just its symptom, and what we in the advertising community can do about it.

The latest Harris poll findings, as I interpret them, identify the underlying cause of today's problems as faulty communication. As a result, public confidence has fallen to its lowest point in many years. The public believes that business and government is simply out of touch with them. The majority of people believe they are being treated as though they had a 12-year-old mentality. We know in the ad business, it is a fatal error to underestimate the consumer's intelligence. Consequently, they have lost confidence in our ability to develop constructive long-term approaches to recession and other issues having to do with the quality of American life.

In my judgment, this loss of faith has been triggered by inflation because it is the root of most of the problems we face —and we have failed to get this point across. Inflation's tentacles reach out in many directions. For example, because the cause and effect relationship of inflation is not generally understood, people do not believe they are getting value for their money in most products they buy today. So, confidence in business—and with it confidence in advertising—declines.

■ No matter what the reasons for inflation, the business man (and he is the advertiser) is at the end of the line. It is he who has the unhappy chore of jacking up prices to the consumer—and with the increases, confidence goes out the window. Because apparently the public has erroneously concluded the advertiser profits from inflated prices.

It is rather shocking to learn that our customers, the public, estimate that the average manufacturer—and he is the advertiser—makes somewhere around 28¢ out of every dollar of sales *after* taxes. Actually, in good times, he realizes about 4¢! So in fact, the public believes that business profits are some seven times greater than they actually are. No wonder public confidence has eroded. No wonder the job of advertising is a tough one.

BY STANLEY I. TANNENBAUM
Chairman of the Board, Kenyon & Eckhardt, New York

One of our main communications tasks, therefore, in restoring confidence in business is to put profits in better perspective in the public's mind with business' cost of *doing business*. And that calls for corporate advertising and public relations programs that tackle the problem head on.

■ Too much of our advertising is incestuous. We are preoccupied with what we want to say when we should be telling the public what it wants to know.

The challenge is there, but so far the response has been weak. By default we have allowed business' critics—and they are the real critics of advertising—to preempt the role of communicator. These politically active destroyers of confidence ignore the benefits of our free enterprise system while pointing out only its faults. We call them "militants" because they promote their thinking with unrelenting vigor, while the average business executive is so repelled by politics he refuses to become personally involved.

It is a rare business man who has a comprehensive plan to present to help restore faith in ourselves, despite the fact that business men generally have a deep down belief in the benefits that business provides to all our people. But how many make the effort to "sell" America on the system that built America? No wonder there has been a loss of confidence. Fortunately for us, the American public has a great deal of common sense. They have

a subconscious understanding that comes from experience; give them the facts and they will come to the right conclusion.

■ What can we do as professional communicators to awaken this subconscious awareness into a new spirit of national confidence? We have, within our means, the ability to make the restoration of confidence in government the guiding spirit of our nation's Bicentennial. And if we can do that, confidence in business will be its by-product.

It seems to me we have to provide the direction. American business developed its world-envied efficiency by planning. Many of you have been engaged in the development of marketing plans for business. We, the advertising community, should make it our business now to see to it that government has a communications plan to restore confidence. Not a Democratic plan. Not a Republican plan. But an all-American Bicentennial confidence-building plan.

As we know, any worth while marketing plan includes goals and priorities along with measurement provisions for standards of performance. Too often, government officials use the marketing vocabulary in explaining their aims, but the execution is faulty. The basics are overlooked.

■ If that appears to be an unkind observation, let me give you a simple but graphic analogy: Let's call our country U.S.A. Inc. Suppose in developing the marketing plan for U.S.A. Inc., we identified our major problem:

The reason we were not selling more of our products was because the consumer had lost interest: Consumers had grown so apathetic that 45% of them wouldn't even walk down the supermarket aisle to look at our merchandise.

■ We would do something about it, wouldn't we? Well, U.S.A. Inc. has that problem. And it's largely being ignored. Forty-five per cent of the electorate didn't bother to vote in the last national election. Why? We ought to find out. If they didn't like candidate No. 1, or No. 2, did we give them an opportunity to register a vote indicating their rejection of the choice given them? We do in-market-

An early outdoor poster (about 1915) for Kellogg's corn flakes told its story simply, with package prominent.

ing research. The respondent can vote "yes" or "no" or "neither." And if the "neithers" were to register 45% of the total, we would quickly decide something was wrong.

But it is probably not that simple. So let's pursue the subject further. If 45% of the electorate doesn't vote, maybe it's not all attributable to apathy. Maybe November is just a bum month for a national election. Why November? Possibly more people would come out in the spring when the days are sunnier and longer in more parts of the country. And just possibly more people would show their interest on April 15, when their income tax filing date comes due. At that time, they might be a little more conscious of their financing of "pie-in-the-sky" programs others have been deciding for them.

■ The fact is, we do not know much about the underlying causes of voter apathy—an apathy which distinguishes us from the active voter participation in other democracies. Nor do we know much about public sentiment in a number of other areas related to confidence which the execution of a national marketing plan could bring into focus.

In the development of a national marketing plan, we would begin with a self examination. For example, what is our national image? How do the shareholders of U.S.A. Inc. view the corporation today vs. last year or five years ago? Any successful corporation knows how the public, its customers and shareholders regard it. And they track changes in sentiment over a period of time so they can anticipte problems and opportunities and move to meet them. They are not always successful, but their failures are rarely the result of ignorance.

I doubt if we ever would have had an

oil crisis if U.S.A. Inc. had had a long-term marketing plan, for we would have considered our resources, our projected rate of consumption, our sources of supply and what was required to maintain and develop them. Without a plan, we were jolted by a "surprise" engergy crisis. (One leading advertiser says, "The best surprise . . . is no surprise.")

■ I also doubt if we would be having today's crisis of confidence if we knew what our national image was and could identify its pluses and minuses, for we would have determined who we are, what

Boy, those Maytag people! They must stay up nights thinking of ways to keep a Maytag Repairman lonely!

MAYTAG
THE DEPENDABILITY PEOPLE

Big marketing success of the decade has been Maytag's campaign featuring a "lonely" repairman who bemoans the lack of service need on the brand of laundry/-kitchen units, and tells why.

we are selling and to whom we are selling it.

There is a need to establish national goals and priorities which reflect our character and our determination. And these have to be communicated so the public understands and appreciates them. And here the management of U.S.A. Inc. might well adopt a basic advertising principle:

Every major policy communication should be considered as a contribution to the complex symbol which is the U.S.A.'s brand image. As such, they can build one on the other toward a long-term objective:

Hit and run—and contradictory pronouncements of national purpose—can be no more effective in building confidence in U.S.A. Inc. than one-shot efforts for an advertiser. The successful brands in America (they have also become successful internationally) become so because they built a coherent brand image in their advertising communications over a period of years. They stood for something specific and kept it on the communication rails.

■ Think of all the forces at work to change the personality and image of a brand, be it for Ivory soap or U.S.A. Inc. Ad managers . . . *they* come and go. Congressmen . . . *they* come and go. Copywriters . . . *they* come and go. Senators . . . *they* come and go. It takes determination and a marketing plan with a coherent strategy to fight off all the diverse pressures for consistent change in direction.

But prosperity is there for the corporation with the brains to create a favorable brand image for its product and to constantly develop it.

The companies who developed the

communications strategy that built the brand images for Ivory soap, Marlboro cigarets, Ford Motor Co.'s cars and Campbell Soup understood that newspaper ads, radio and tv commercials are not one-time shots to zig-zag and flip-flop at personal whims of the moment, but long-term investments in their brands' total personality.

Why can't U.S.A. Inc. adopt this strategy? Wouldn't it be a way to build confidence in the U.S.A. brand? American business with its components that make up U.S.A. Inc. was built that way.

Feelings and attitudes are crucial in instilling conviction and confidence not only for products, but for nations. And the best way for our country to go forward is to learn more about the attitudes of our people.

Suppose a representative sample of people received an attitude questionnaire with their income tax form which they could return anonymously in a separate prepaid envelope. I think Uncle Sam would get a good return, at the moment of truth, at the time the respondent was computing *his* cost of government.

I suggest it be made a national marketing requisite that our legislators reflecting the attitudes and feelings of the public chisel in granite a definition of the image which they wish the U.S.A. brand to acquire over the years.

Once this is determined, it will be less easy for changing office-holders to blur the image each in his own fashion. The public deserves a definition of the U.S.A. brand image. It should be restated to them at frequent intervals. Our legislators who work with it should understand it and stick to it. While their pronounce-

A coupon ad in 1909 looked like this in The Saturday Evening Post. It was run by B. J. Johnson Soap Co. for Palmolive soap, offering a free bar with coupon.

ments can and should change in light of debate and domestic international considerations, the U.S.A. brand image should hold firm.

Blurred images don't inspire consumer confidence and I submit that the loss of confidence reported in the Harris and other opinion polls depicts a wishy-washy image—the result of constantly changing directions.

■ David Ogilvy, commenting on brand images, once made the observation that no capon ever ruled the roost. Our national symbol is the American eagle. To what virtue does it trigger the mind? I

was taught the eagle was pretty confident of its power, its courage, and its tenacity.

In rebuilding confidence, it seems to me that the displined thinking inherent in successful marketing must be more directly applied to government. This suggests the need for a marketing director—at the cabinet officer level: A secretary of communications.

He would be the focal point of government communications both internally and with the private sector. A secretary of communications would supervise the annual reporting of our national goals and their assigned priorities together with the estimated costs and resources available to meet them. His principal objective would be to see that *we are not surprised.*

The public does not want to be surprised. They can accept adversity along with prosperity, provided they know where they stand and why. Annual reports citing goals and progress made toward achievement from a secretary of communications would rivet the public's attention on the gap between what we want and what we can afford while also providing a report card on government's performance.

Systemized "reporting" and "corekeeping" are demanded by both business and labor in their respective organizations. Confidence in business and labor leadership is maintained by their ability to cite progress to their shareholders and membership against specific and measureable benchmarks. The maintenance of citizen confidence in government performance is no less demanding. #

Bicentennial collection: The 'best ads I've ever seen'

Name "the best ads or ad campaigns that you've ever seen or heard." That request was put by ADVERTISING AGE to 97 advertising professionals. In response, they nominated 200 or more ads and campaigns, reflecting some diversity but much unanimity.

About 50 of these nominations got more votes than all the others. A remarkable accolade was accorded Doyle Dane Bernbach's campaign for Volkswagen: It received the votes of 60 of the 97 panelists.

The runner-up was Leo Burnett's campaign for Marlboro and Marlboro Country, which won the approval of 28 panelists. In third place was Coca-Cola's famous hilltop commercial, created by McCann-Erickson, which garnered 24 votes. Next was BBDO's advertising for Campbell Soup and the Campbell Soup Kids, which won the approval of 22 judges.

The remainder of the top ten ads (including ties) were Ogilvy's Hathaway shirt effort; Doyle Dane's Alka-Seltzer campaign; Foote, Cone & Belding's "Does she or doesn't she?" for Clairol; John Caples' "They Laughed When I Sat Down at the Piano"; Ogilvy's Rolls-Royce ad, "At 60 miles per hour . . . ," and Doyle Dane's No. 2 efforts for Avis.

Uncola and 'Look at All Three'

The next most popular ten with the panelists (including ties) were J. Walter Thompson's Uncola campaign for Seven-Up; McDonald's hamburgers, by Needham, Harper & Steers; Needham's Xerox advertising; Young & Rubicam's Jell-O advertising (Jack Benny and Bill Cosby); Sterling Getchell's classic "Look at All 3" for Plymouth; Lambert & Feasley's halitosis, "Always a Bridesmaid" and "Best Friend Won't Tell You" efforts for Listerine; BBDO's Pepsi-Cola advertising; Ogilvy's Schweppes (with Comdr.

Whitehead); William H. Weintraub's Fire & Ice campaign for Revlon. Also, BBDO's Lucky Strike advertising (including L-S-M-F-T); Benton & Bowles' Instant Maxwell House copy ("tiny flavor buds"), Compton's advertising for Ivory soap; "The Kid In Upper 4," written for the New Haven Rail Road by Nelson C. Metcalf Jr., and Kraft's tv advertising by J. Walter Thompson.

Close behind were United Airlines' Friendly Skies by Leo Burnett Co.; Young & Rubicam's Bert & Harry output for Piel's beer; Ohrbach's advertising by Doyle Dane Bernbach; "Nobody but Nobody Undersells Gimbel's," by Bernice Fitz-Gibbon; BBDO's "When you're having more than one" advertising for Schaefer beer; Ogilvy's Mercedes advertising; J. Walter Thompson's campaigns for Lux soap; Kenyon & Eckhardt's "A Hog Can Cross the Country Without Changing Trains—But YOU Can't!" for

Think small.

Ten years ago, the first Volkswagens were imported into the United States.

These strange little cars with their beetle shapes were almost unknown.

All they had to recommend them was 32 miles to the gallon (regular gas, regular driving), an aluminum air-cooled rear engine that would go 70 mph all day without strain, sensible size for a family and a sensible price-tag too.

Beetles multiply; so do Volkswagens. By 1954,

VW was the best-selling imported car in America. It has held that rank each year since. In 1959, over 150,000 Volkswagens were sold, including 30,000 station wagons and trucks.

Volkswagen's snub nose is now familiar in fifty states of the Union; as American as apple strudel. In fact, your VW may well be made with Pittsburgh steel stamped out on Chicago presses (even the power for the Volkswagen plant is supplied by coal from the U.S.A.).

As any VW owner will tell you, Volkswagen service is excellent and it is everywhere. Parts are plentiful, prices low. (A new fender, for example, is only $21.75.*) No small factor in Volkswagen's success.

Today, in the U.S.A. and 119 other countries, Volkswagens are sold faster than they can be made. Volkswagen has become the world's fifth largest automotive manufacturer by thinking small. More and more people are thinking the same. *Suggested retail price.

Leading all others in votes for "best I've ever seen" was the Volkswagen campaign.

97 who named 'best ads I've ever seen'

Peter W. Allport, Assn. of National Advertisers
Prof. Kenward L. Atkin, California State University

Howard H. Bell, American Advertising Federation
Brown Bolte, Realty Enterprises Corp.
Del Bowman, Hughes Aircraft Co.
Prof. Robert S. Boyd, Virginia Commonwealth University
Steuart Henderson Britt, Britt & Frerichs Inc.
Charles H. Brower, BBDO (ret.)
Sanford Buchsbaum, Revlon
Budd Buszek, Traffic Audit Bureau

Norman E. Cash, Television Bureau of Advertising
John Caples, BBDO
Gene Case, Case & McGrath Inc.
William J. Colihan, Criterion Advertising Co.
Barton A. Cummings, Compton Advertising
Joseph W. Curran, RCA

Maxwell Dane, Doyle Dane Bernbach (ret.)
Miles David, Radio Advertising Bureau
Robert F. DeLay, Direct Mail/Marketing Assn.

Mauri Edwards, Foster Grant Co.

Arthur C. Fatt, Grey Advertising
Robert L. Ficks Jr., Ethan Allen Inc.
Clifford L. Fitzgerald, Dancer-Fitzgerald-Sample Inc.
Paul Foley, Interpublic Group of Cos.
Archibald McG. Foster, Ted Bates & Co.
Jo Foxworth, Jo Foxworth Inc.
Prof. Vernon Fryburger, Northwestern University

Prof. John W. Garberson, University of Nevada
Ross R. Garrett, 3M Co.
Prof. Stephen A. Greyser, Harvard Business School

Thomas C. Harrison, Blair Radio
Sandy Alan Haver, Colgate-Palmolive Co.
Robert E. Healy, Interpublic Group of Cos.
Fred W. Heckel, United Airlines
Prof. Conrad R. Hill, University of Rhode Island
Whit Hobbs, The New Yorker
Harold W. Hoffman, U.S. Steel Corp.
Marvin Honig, Doyle Dane Bernbach Inc.
Henry Hunter, Olin Corp.

Eugene D. Jackson, National Black Network
Prof. Richard Joel, University of Tennessee
Tad Jeffery, Florida Citrus Commission

Jack Kauffman, Newspaper Advertising Bureau
Otto Kleppner, author
A. O. Knowlton, General Foods Corp.
Lois Korey, Needham, Harper & Steers
Reva Korda, Ogilvy & Mather
Eugene H. Kummel, McCann-Erickson Worldwide

Prof. James E. Littlefield, University of North Carolina

Richard J. Lord, Lord, Geller, Federico Inc.

William A. Marsteller, Marsteller Inc.
Edward A. McCabe, Scali, McCabe, Sloves Inc.
James McCaffrey, McCaffrey & McCall (ret.)
J. Robert McMenamin, Uniroyal Inc.
Charles S. Mill, American Business Press
Charles Moss, Wells, Rich, Greene Inc.
Arthur H. Motley, Parade
Prof. John G. Myers, University of California, Berkeley

Robert D. Nelson, Los Angeles Times
Edward N. Ney, Young & Rubicam International
Eugene F. Novak, Rumrill-Hoyt Inc.

Neal W. O'Connor, N W Ayer ABH International
David Ogilvy, Ogilvy & Mather
John E. O'Toole, Foote, Cone & Belding

Ed Parets, Schenley Affiliated Brands Corp.
Prof. Franklin N. Pierce, University of Florida
Donald G. Pojednic, Foote, Cone & Belding
Shirley Polykoff, Shirley Polykoff Advertising
Chester L. Posey, de Garmo Inc.

Prof. Michael L. Ray, Stanford University
Roger D. Rice, Television Bureau of Advertising
Rosser Reeves, Rosser Reeves Inc.
Raymond Rubicam, Young & Rubicam (ret.)

Harry F. Schroeter, Nabisco (ret.)
Prof. Ernest A. Sharpe, University of Texas at Austin

Thomas R. Shepard Jr., Institute of Outdoor Advertising
Jerry J. Siano, N W Ayer ABH International
Otto A. Silha, Minneapolis Star & Tribune Co.
Len Sirowitz, Rosenfeld, Sirowitz & Lawson Inc.
William Sharp, Coca-Cola USA
Prof. Jack Z. Sissors, Northwestern University
John J. Slaven, Volkswagen of America

F. L. Smawley, Jos. Schlitz Brewing Co.
C. R. Standen, Tatham-Laird & Kudner
Prof. Edward Stephens, Northwestern University
Kenneth Stuart, Reader's Digest

Stanley I. Tannenbaum, Kenyon & Eckhardt
Jack G. Thayer, NBC Radio Division
Samuel Thurm, Assn. of National Advertisers
Jane Trahey, Trahey/Rogers Advertising
William D. Tyler, creative consultant and columnist

Prof. Stephen Unwin, University of Alabama

John P. Warwick, Warwick, Welsh & Miller
Vincent T. Wasilewski, National Assn. of Broadcasters
Walter Weir, consultant
Edward B. Wilson, J. Walter Thompson Co.
Lois Wyse, Wyse Advertising

the Chesapeake & Ohio Railway; Sunkist advertising by Foote, Cone & Belding and its early predecessor agency Lord & Thomas.

Breathless Smirnoff, Ford in Future

In the next group were Leo Burnett's Green Giant campaign; Camel cigarets' "I'd walk a mile," by N W Ayer; Leo Burnett's Kellogg advertising ("Best to You Each Morning"); Ajax foaming cleanser by McCann-Erickson; the "Ford in Your Future" campaign by J. Walter Thompson; Doyle Dane Bernbach's output for Polaroid and Chivas Regal; Ogilvy & Mather's "Tread softly past the long, long sleep of kings" for the British Travel Assn.; "Do You Make These Mistakes in English" by Ruthrauff & Ryan (Maxwell Sackheim); Ted Bates' campaign for Anacin; "My friend, Joe Holmes, is now a Horse" by Young & Rubicam (George Gribbin) for Arrow Shirts; the Lawrence C. Gumbinner "It leaves you breathless" campaign for Smirnoff vodka; and American Airlines' advertising by Doyle Dane Bernbach.

Other outstanding ads and campaigns:

De Beers (N W Ayer).

Cadillac "Penalty of Leadership" (MacManus, John & Adams).

Maidenform "I dreamed . . ." (Norman, Craig & Kummel).

Exxon (McCaffrey & McCall).

Hallmark Hall of Fame (Foote, Cone & Belding).

Hamm's beer (Campbell-Mithun).

Modess (Young & Rubicam).

Scoring high behind the Volkswagen campaign for "best ever" votes were the Campbell kids campaign (above) and the Coca-Cola hilltop commercial shown on the opposite page. Close behind the top ten was McDonald's, as indicated by the scene, below, from one of the chain's commercials.

On a hilltop in Italy,
We assembled young people
From all over the world...
To bring you this message
From Coca-Cola Bottlers
All over the world!
It's the real thing. Coke.

As indicated, **this Coca-Cola commercial** in its "real thing" campaign garnered third place in the voting. In sixth place was the Doyle Dane campaign for Alka-Seltzer, with the eager young bride fixing concoctions which her husband dutifully (and distressingly) ate and praised.

"Can he really play?" a girl whispered. "Heavens no!" Arthur exclaimed. "He never played a note in his life."

They Laughed When I Sat Down At the Piano
But When I Started to Play!—

ARTHUR had just played "The Rosary." The room rang with applause. I decided that this would be a dramatic moment for me to make my debut. To the amazement of all my friends, I strode confidently over to the piano and sat down.

"Jack is up to his old tricks," somebody chuckled. The crowd laughed. They were all certain that I couldn't play a single note.

"Can he really play?" I heard a girl whisper to Arthur.

"Heavens, no!" Arthur exclaimed—"He never played a note in all his life. . . But just you watch him. This is going to be good."

I decided to make the most of the situation. With mock dignity I drew out a silk handkerchief and lightly dusted off the piano keys. Then I rose and gave the revolving piano stool a quarter of a turn, just as I had seen an imitator of Paderewski do in a vaudeville sketch.

"What do you think of his execution?" called a voice from the rear.

"We're in favor of it!" came back the answer, and the crowd rocked with laughter.

Then I Started to Play

Instantly a tense silence fell on the guests. The laughter died on their lips as if by magic. I played through the first few bars of Beethoven's immortal Moonlight Sonata. I heard gasps of amazement. My friends sat breathless—spellbound!

I played on and as I played I forgot the people around me. I forgot the hour, the place, the breathless listeners. The little world I lived in seemed to fade—seemed to grow dim—unreal. Only the music was real. Only the music and visions it brought me. Visions as beautiful and as changing as the wind blown clouds and drifting moonlight that long ago inspired the master composer. It seemed as if the master

musician himself were speaking to me—speaking through the medium of music—not in words but in chords. Not in sentences but in exquisite melodies!

A Complete Triumph!

As the last notes of the Moonlight Sonata died away, the room resounded with a sudden roar of applause. I found myself surrounded by excited faces. How my friends carried on! Men shook my hand—wildly congratulated me—pounded me on the back in their enthusiasm! Everybody was exclaiming with delight—plying me with rapid questions. . . "Jack! Why didn't you tell us you could play like that?". . . "Where did you learn?"—"How long have you studied?"—"Who was your teacher?"

"I have never even seen my teacher," I replied. "And just a short while ago I couldn't play a note.".

"Quit your kidding," laughed Arthur, himself an accomplished pianist. "You've been studying for years. I can tell."

"I have been studying only a short while," I insisted. "I decided to keep it a secret so that I could surprise all you folks."

Then I told them the whole story.

"Have you ever heard of the U. S. School of Music?" I asked.

A few of my friends nodded. "That's a correspondence school, isn't it?" they exclaimed.

"Exactly," I replied. "They have a new simplified method that can teach you to play any instrument by mail in just a few months."

How I Learned to Play Without a Teacher

And then I explained how for years I had longed to play the piano.

"A few months ago," I continued, "I saw an interesting ad for the U. S. School of Music—a new method of learning to play with only cost a few cents a day! The ad told how a woman had mastered the piano in her spare time at home—and without a teacher! Best of all, the wonderful new method she used, required no laborious scales—no heartless exercises — no tiresome practising. It sounded so convincing that I filled out the coupon requesting the Free Demonstration Lesson.

"The free book arrived promptly and I started in that very night to study the Demonstration Lesson. I was amazed to see how easy it was to play this new way. Then I sent for the course.

"When the course arrived I found it was just as the ad said — as easy as A.B.C! And, as

the lessons continued they got easier and easier. Before I knew it I was playing all the pieces I liked best. Nothing stopped me. I could play ballads or classical numbers or jazz, all with equal ease! And I never did have any special talent for music!"

Play Any Instrument

You too, can now teach yourself to be an accomplished musician—right at home—in half the usual time. You can't go wrong with this simple new method which has already shown 350,000 people how to play their favorite instruments. Forget that old-fashioned idea that you need special "talent." Just read the list of instruments in the panel, decide which one you want to play, and the U. S. School will do the rest. And bear in mind no matter which instrument you choose, the cost in each case will be the same—just a few cents a day. No matter whether you are a mere beginner or already a good performer, you will be interested in learning about this new and wonderful method.

Send for Our Free Booklet and Demonstration Lesson

Thousands of successful students never dreamed they possessed musical ability until it was revealed to them by a remarkable "Musical Ability Test" which we send entirely without cost with our interesting free booklet.

If you are in earnest about wanting to play your favorite instrument—if you really want to gain happiness and increase your popularity—send at once for the free booklet and Demonstration Lesson. No cost — no obligation. Right now we are making a Special offer for a limited number of new students. Sign and send the convenient coupon now—before it's too late to gain the benefits of this offer. Instruments supplied when needed, cash or credit. U. S. School of Music, 1031 Brunswick Bldg., New York City.

Pick Your Instrument

Piano	'Cello
Organ	Harmony and Composition
Violin	Sight Singing
Drums and Traps	Ukulele
Banjo	Guitar
Tenor Banjo	Hawaiian Steel Guitar
Mandolin	Harp
Clarinet	Cornet
Flute	Piccolo
Saxophone	Trombone
Voice and Speech Culture	
Automatic Finger Control	
Piano Accordion	

U. S. School of Music,
1031 Brunswick Bldg., New York City.

Please send me your free book, "Music Lessons in Your Own Home," with introduction by Dr. Frank Crane, Demonstration Lesson and particulars of your Special Offer. I am interested in the following course:

....

Have you above instrument? ....

Name ....
(Please write plainly)

Address ....

City .... State............

An alltime great, John Caples' famous ad, "They Laughed When I sat Down . . ." was another one voted in Ad Age's top ten. Mr. Caples wrote it back in 1925.

Mobil safety campaign (Doyle Dane Bernbach).

Bulova Watch (Biow Co.).

Book of Etiquette (Ruthrauff & Ryan).

Colgate Dental Cream (Ted Bates & Co.).

Charmin tissue (Benton & Bowles).

Perdue chickens (Scali, McCabe, Sloves).

Sears, Roebuck (Ogilvy & Mather and Foote, Cone & Belding).

Crest toothpaste (Benton & Bowles).

Chevrolet "See the U.S.A. . . ." (Campbell-Ewald).

Levy's bread (Doyle Dane Bernbach).

Hamilton Watch (BBDO).

Philip Morris "Call for . . ." (Biow Co.).

Shell (Ogilvy & Mather).

Squibb "Priceless ingredient" (N W Ayer—by Ray Rubicam).

Volvo (Scali, McCabe, Sloves).

Puerto Rico (Ogilvy & Mather).

El Al Airlines (Doyle Dane Bernbach).

Macy's (Bernice Fitz-Gibbon).

Gimbel's "Nobody but nobody" (Bernice Fitz-Gibbon).

Life Savers (Young & Rubicam).

Pond's "She's engaged . . ." (J. Walter Thompson).

Charles Atlas "97-lb. weakling" (Schwab & Beatty).

Container Corp. "Great Ideas of Western Man" (N W Ayer).

Del Monte "Cosby commercials" (McCann-Erickson).

Cutty Sark (Lois Holland Callaway).

Barney's Men's Store (Griswold-Eshleman).

Eastern Airlines (Young & Rubicam).

Maxwell House (perking pot) (Ogilvy & Mather).

M&M Candy "Melts in your mouth" (Ted Bates & Co.).

Kool cigarets (Ted Bates & Co.).

MEN WANTED for hazardous journey. Small wages, bitter cold, long months of complete darkness, constant danger, safe return doubtful. Honor and recognition in case of success.—Ernest Shackleton.

These were choices of 97 ad pundits. Another 97 might have included a few other classics, but surely would have named just about all those cited here.

Bicentennial collection: The 'best ads I've ever seen'

Bicentennial 'best ads'

Second highest in votes for "the best ad or campaign I've ever seen" was the durable Marlboro campaign. In the top five was the classic "The man in the Hathaway shirt" campaign which ran for years and starred the famous eyepatch, even making the model something of a celebrity. Also scoring high was the striking Revlon Fire and Ice campaign, Lucky Strike with slogan, "L.S.M.F.T." and the famous "Man from Schweppes."

The man in the Hathaway shirt

AMERICAN MEN are beginning to realize that it is ridiculous to buy good suits and then spoil the effect by wearing an ordinary, mass-produced shirt. Hence the growing popularity of HATHAWAY shirts, which are in a class by themselves.

HATHAWAY shirts *wear* infinitely longer—a matter of years. They make you look younger and more distinguished, because of the subtle way HATHAWAY cut collars. The whole shirt is tailored more *generously*, and is therefore more *comfortable*. The tails are longer, and stay in your trousers. The buttons are mother-of-pearl. Even the stitching has an ante-bellum elegance about it.

Above all, HATHAWAY make their shirts of remarkable *fabrics*, collected from the four corners of the earth—Viyella and Aertex, from England, woolen taffeta from Scotland, Sea Island cotton from the West Indies, hand-woven madras from India, broadcloth from Manchester, linen batiste from Paris, hand-blocked silks from England, exclusive cottons from the best weavers in America. You will get a great deal of quiet satisfaction out of wearing shirts which are in such impeccable taste.

HATHAWAY shirts are made by a small company of dedicated craftsmen in the little town of Waterville, Maine. They have been at it, man and boy, for one hundred and twenty years.

At better stores everywhere, or write C. F. HATHAWAY, Waterville, Maine, for the name of your nearest store. In New York, telephone OX 7-5566. Prices from $5.95 to $20.00.

HATHAWAY SHIRTS

REVLON

Smoke a LUCKY to feel your LEVEL best!

Luckies' fine tobacco picks you up when you're low . . . calms you down when you're tense!

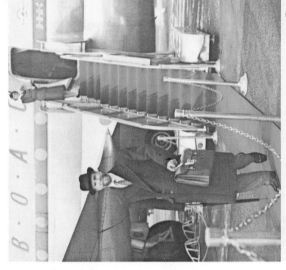

The man from Schweppes is here

SCHWEPPES

LUCKY STRIKE

Come to where the flavor is. Marlboro

Marlboro Red or Longhorn 100's— you got a lot to like.

Warning: The Surgeon General Has Determined That Cigarette Smoking Is Dangerous to Your Health.

MARLBORO

Bicentennial 'best ads'

The memorable Rolls-Royce ad and the Avis "We're only No. 2" campaign landed in AA top ten, "Often a Bridesmaid" top 20.

"At 60 miles an hour the loudest noise in this new Rolls-Royce comes from the electric clock"

What makes Rolls-Royce the best car in the world? "There is really no magic about it—it is merely patient attention to detail," says an eminent Rolls-Royce engineer.

The Rolls-Royce Silver Cloud $13,550

Avis is only No.2 in rent a cars. So why go with us?

We try harder.

(When you're not the biggest, you have to.)

We just can't afford dirty ash-trays. Or half-empty gas tanks. Or worn wipers. Or unwashed cars. Or low tires. Or anything less than seat-adjusters that adjust. Heaters that heat. Defrost-

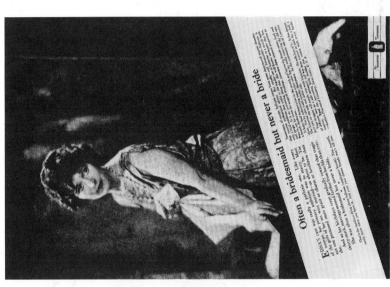

Often a bridesmaid but never a bride

When **David Ogilvy** wrote this Rolls-Royce ad, he worked in more than a great headline. He used long copy, including 19 big product advantages—and the price, too.

Doyle Dane Bernbach's clever "Only No. 2" campaign for Avis dumped the overused "We're the greatest" theme of adland, caught notice, enhanced believability.

See the Rolls-Royce and Bentley at Stand 13, International Automobile Show, New York Coliseum, April 5-13.

A crusade to improve railroad service got a boost from the above 1945 ad. The famous Listerine ad ran in the '20s, Cadillac's ran just once, in early 1915.

A Hog Can Cross the Country Without Changing Trains—But YOU Can't!

The Chesapeake & Ohio Railway and the Nickel Plate Road are again proposing to give human beings a break!

It's hard to believe, but it's true.

If you want to ship a hog from coast to coast, he can make the entire trip without changing cars. You can't. It is impossible for you to pass through Chicago, St. Louis, or New Orleans without breaking your trip!

There is an invisible barrier down the middle of the United States which you cannot cross without inconvenience, lost time, and trouble.

If you want to board a sleeper on one coast and ride through to the other, you must make double Pullman reservations, pack and transfer your baggage, often change stations, and wait around for connections.

It's the same sad story if you make a relatively short trip. You can't cross that mysterious line! To go from Fort Wayne to Milwaukee or from Cleveland to Des Moines, you must also stop and change trains.

Last year alone, more than 560,000 people were forced to make annoying, time-wasting stopovers at the phantom Chinese wall which splits America in half!

Why should travel be less convenient for people than it is for pigs? Why should Americans be denied the benefits of through train service? No one has yet been able to explain it.

Canada has this service . . . with a choice

of two routes. Canada isn't split down the middle. Why should we be? No reasonable answer has yet been given. Passengers still have to stop off at Chicago, St. Louis, and New Orleans—although they can ride right through other important rail centers.

It's time to pry the lid off this mystery. It's time for action to end this inconvenience to the travelling public . . . NOW!

Many railroads could cooperate to provide this needed through service. To date, the Chesapeake & Ohio and the Nickel Plate ALONE have made a public offer to do so.

How about it!

Once more we would like to go on record with this specific proposal:

The **Chesapeake & Ohio**, whose western passenger terminus is Cincinnati, stands ready now to join with any combination of other railroads to set up connecting transcontinental and intermediate service through Chicago and St. Louis, on practical schedules and routes.

The **Nickel Plate Road**, which runs to Chicago and St. Louis, also stands ready now to join with any combination of roads to set up the same kind of connecting service through these two cities.

Through railroad service can't be blocked forever. The public wants it. It's bound to come. Again, we invite the support of the public, of railroad people and railroad investors, for this vitally needed improvement in rail transportation!

Chesapeake & Ohio Railway · Nickel Plate Road

Terminal Tower, Cleveland 1, Ohio

---

nice. To start you out right with a new car, like a lively, super-torque Ford, and a pleasant smile. To let you know, say, where you can get a good, hot pastrami sandwich in Des Moines.

Why?

Because we can't afford to take you for granted.

Go with us next time.

The line at our counter is shorter.

5. There is no multi-metal contact between the body of the car and the chassis frame—except for the speedometer drive. The entire body is insulated and under-sealed.

6. The finished car spends a week in the final test shop, being fine-tuned. Here it is subjected to nearly eight separate tests. For example, the engineers use a stethoscope to listen for axle-whine.

7. The Rolls-Royce is guaranteed for three years. With a new network of dealers and parts-depots from

amount of effort. It relieves you to do just one job. No chauffeur required.

12. The seats are upholstered with eight hides of English leather—enough to make 128 pairs of soft shoes.

13. A picnic table, veneered in French walnut, slides out from under the dash. Two more swing out behind the front seats.

14. You can get such optional extras as an Espresso coffee-making machine, a dictating machine, a bed, hot and cold water for washing, an electric razor.

19. By comparison, the most expensive Rolls-Royce costs...

See the Rolls-Royce and Bentley at Stand 13, International Automobile Show, New York Coliseum, April 5-13.

Bicentennial 'best ads'

Among the top ten "best ads or campaigns" of all time in the voting was the indelible Clairol campaign with its tantalizing headline and wholesome models giving respectability to hair color. High on the list also are United Airlines' Friendly Skies and Kellogg's "Best to you each morning," followed by Polaroid's consistent output and the Sears drive through the years for a new class image.

Does she...or doesn't she?

Hair color so natural only her hairdresser knows for sure!™

Are mothers getting younger or do they just look that way? She, for one, has that fresh, wholesome quality, the bright and shining hair that just naturally keeps a woman looking prettier, younger—as though she's found the secret of making time stand still. And in

a way she has. It's with Miss Clairol, the most effective way to cover gray hair and to revitalize or brighten fading tones. Keeps your hair so soft and lively—in wonderful condition—because Miss Clairol carries the color deep into the hair shaft to shine

outward the way your own color does. That's why Miss Clairol always looks so natural. And that's why hairdressers everywhere recommend it and more women use it than all other haircolorings. Try Miss Clairol yourself. Today. So quick and easy, you'll love it.

MISS CLAIROL

Polaroid invents The SX-70.

Polaroid

Polaroid's SX-70 explained.

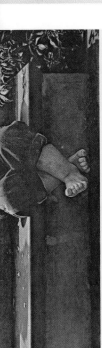

"Look at All THREE!"

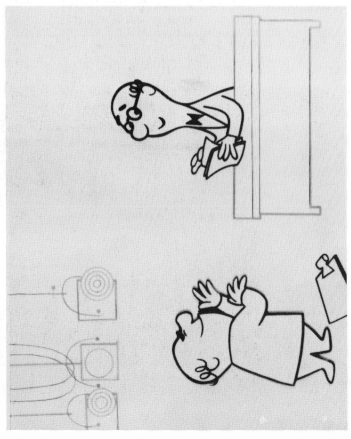

Bicentennial 'best ads'

Picked among the top 25 "best ads": Bert & Harry for Piel's beer.

One of the favorites was this 1932 ad, which boosted Plymouth, until then a small competitor of Ford and Chevrolet.

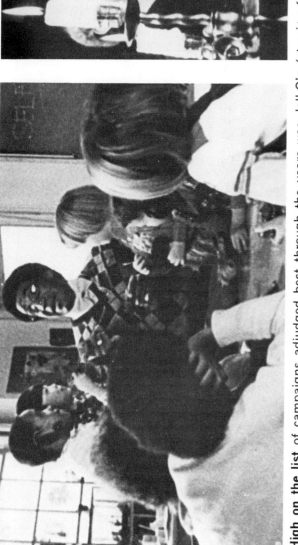

High on the list of campaigns adjudged best through the years was Jell-O's (starring first Jack Benny and later Bill Cosby) and more recently, Xerox's.

Comparable in a sense with Avis' "We're No. 2" is 7Up's "Uncola" campaign, getting many "best ads" votes, along with Kraft's tv advertising.

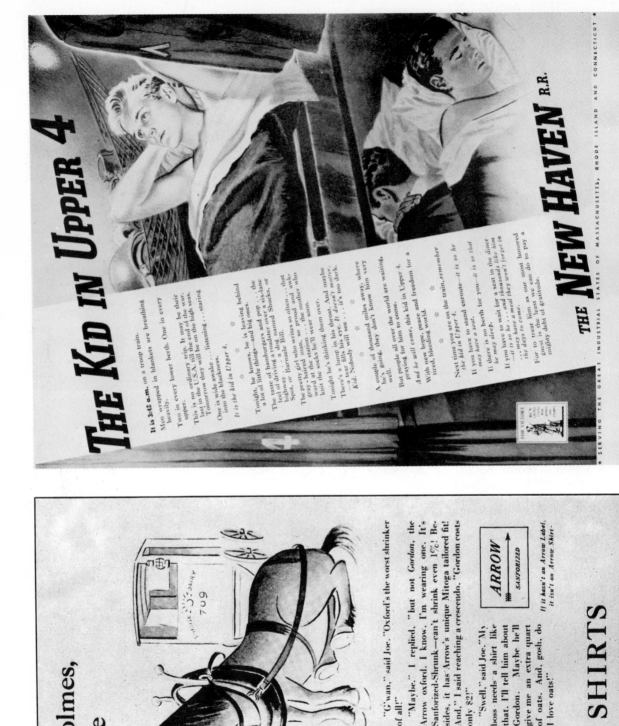

In World War II, this powerful ad eased public discontent with railroads.

In a bygone era, copywriter George Gribbin's whimsy sold Arrow shirts.

Bicentennial 'best ads'

This **top slogan** for Ford incorporated the advertiser's name—no chance to forget it—in a top ad, unlike "Ask the man who owns one."

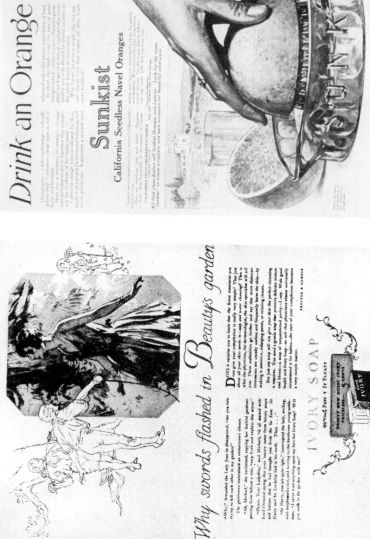

Drink an Orange

Sunkist
California Seedless Navel Oranges

Why swords flashed in Beauty's garden

IVORY SOAP

Two for the road.
Regular Pepsi-Cola and Diet Pepsi-Cola.

Non-stop refreshment
for the **Pepsi generation.**

Diet Pepsi for traveling light.
Regular Pepsi to rev up your spirits.

Liveliest drinks ever to come
down the pike.

COME ALIVE! You're in the Pepsi
generation!

Voted among the "best ads" were campaigns for Pepsi-Cola ("You're in the Pepsi generation"), Ivory soap and Sunkist ("Drink an orange" in 1916).

59

Bicentennial 'best ads'

Schaefer

WHEN YOU'RE HAVING MORE THAN ONE

Great sales pitch to heavy beer drinkers helped Schaefer sales and drew votes as a "best ad."

AMAZING COFFEE DISCOVERY!

Not a powder! Not a grind! But millions of tiny 'FLAVOR BUDS' of real coffee...ready to burst instantly into that famous MAXWELL HOUSE FLAVOR!

The only instant coffee with that GOOD-TO-THE-LAST-DROP flavor!

Launch of Instant Maxwell House with "tiny flavor buds" copy brought instant success and scored high with AA panel.

I found out about Joan

The way she talks, you'd think she was in Who's Who. Well! I found out what's what with *her*. Her husband own a bank? Sweetie, not even a bank *account*. Why that palace of theirs has wall-to-wall *mortgages!* And that car? Darling, that's horsepower, *not earning power*. They won it in a fifty-cent raffle! Can you imagine? And those clothes! Of course she *does* dress divinely. But really...a mink stole, and Paris suits, and all those dresses...on *his income?* Well darling, I found out about that too. I just happened to be going her way and I *saw Joan come out of Ohrbach's!*

Ohrbach's

34ᵀᴴ ST. OPP. EMPIRE STATE BLDG. · NEWARK MARKET & HALSEY · "A BUSINESS IN MILLIONS, A PROFIT IN PENNIES"

© 1956 by Ohrbach's, Inc.

An unforgettable ad for Ohrbach's brought the store's message home with wit, power.

60

The Giant's Sweetlets Peas are a little out of the ordinary.

REGULAR PEAS

TINY, TENDER SWEETLETS PEAS

You don't have to be a Giant to see that Sweetlets Peas are smaller than ordinary peas. They're tender, thin-skinned little peas. With a sweet, delicate flavor all their own.

Sweetlets Peas. A little smaller and a little special. With a little savings, too. From the Jolly Green Giant. Ho, ho.

In the ads, Green Giant found a way to say something about peas.

Henry VII, Elizabeth I and Mary Queen of Scots are buried in this chapel.

Tread softly past the long, long sleep of kings

THIS is Henry VII's chapel in Westminster Abbey. These windows have filtered the sun of five centuries. They have also seen the crowning of twenty-two kings.

Three monarchs rest here now. Henry, Elizabeth and Mary. Such are their names in sleep. No titles. No trumpets. The banners hang battle-heavy and becalmed. But still the royal crown remains. *How sat you and 5 pence.*

When you go to Britain, make yourself this promise. Visit at least *one* of the thirty great cathedrals. Their famous names thunder! Durham and Armagh. Or they chime? Lincoln and Canterbury. And sometimes they *whisper.* Wells, Winchester, Norwich and Salisbury.

Take a map and make your choice.

Each cathedral transcends the noblest single work of art. It is a pinnacle of faith and an act of centuries. It is an offering of human hands as close to Abraham as it is to Bach. Listen to the soaring choirs at evensong. And, if you can, go there for Easter.

You will rejoice that you did.

For free color booklet "Cathedrals in Britain," see your travel agent or write Box 194, British Travel Association. In New York—680 Fifth Avenue; In Los Angeles—606 South Hill St.; In Chicago—39 South La Salle St.; In Canada—90 Adelaide Street West, Toronto

Great copy was a strong lure in the British Travel Assn.'s print ad.

Since first straw vote in 1824, research grows

BY JACK J. HONOMICHL

Would anybody guess that marketing research goes back nearly to this country's beginnings?

Well, take political polling. In July, 1824, the *Harrisburg Pennsylvanian* printed a report of a straw vote taken at Wilmington, Del., "without discrimination of parties." In that election year poll, Andrew Jackson received 335 votes; John Quincy Adams, 169; Henry Clay, 19, and William H. Crawford, nine. Later the same year, another newspaper, the *Raleigh Star*, undertook to canvass political meetings held in North Carlina, "at which the sense of the people was taken."

Use of original marketing research by an advertising agency to gain a new account popped up as early as 1879. N. W. Ayer & Son was soliciting the Nichols-Shepard Co., manufacturer of agricultural machinery. Ayer prepared a media schedule which was challenged by the would-be client, according to L. C. Lockley writing in *The Journal of Marketing* for April, 1950. Substantiation came from an Ayer survey of state officials and publishers throughout the country asking for information on grain production and media circulation by counties. The client was impressed and Ayer got the account.

■ In 1895, Harlow Gale of the University of Minnesota was using mailed questionnaires to obtain public opinions on advertising, and George B. Waldron was doing qualitative research for Mahin's Advertising Agency around 1900, according to Mr. Lockley. In 1901, Walter Dill Scott, later president of Northwestern University, undertook a program of experimental research on advertising for the Agate Club of Chicago.

It wasn't until about 1910, according to Mr. Lockley, "that evidences of market research became frequent enough to indicate that a new field of business activity had made a serious start." In 1911, for instance, J. George Frederick left the editorship of *Printer's Ink* to start what may have been the first business research company, the Business Bourse. Among his early clients were General Electric and the Texas Co. By Mr. Frederick's estimates, no more than $50,000 was spent in gathering marketing information, even informally, in 1910.

It was also in 1911 that R. O. Eastman, then advertising manager for the Kellogg Co. in Battle Creek, Mich., interested some members of the Assn. of National Advertising Managers (as the Assn. of National Advertisers was then known) to cooperate on a joint postcard questionnaire survey to determine magazine readership. That introduced the important concept of duplication of circulation. Mr. Eastman became so involved in this sort of survey that in 1916 he started his own company, the Eastman Research Bureau. His first clients were *Cosmopolitan* and the *Christian Herald,* followed later by the General Electric Co., which wanted a consumer survey to determine recognition of the "Mazda" trademark.

The year 1911 also saw the establishment of a Bureau of Business Research at the Harvard Graduate School of Business, as well as the now-famous Commercial Research Division of the Curtis Publishing Co., headed by Charles C. Parlin. This operation was spun off in 1943 to become the company now known as National Analysts. In 1915, the U. S. Rubber Co. started a research department headed by Dr. Paul H. Nystrom, and two years later Swift & Co. followed with a department headed by Dr. Louis D. H. Weld.

In the newspaper field, the *Chicago Tribune* pioneered in 1916 with a door-to-door survey of consumer purchasing habits in Chicago. This same paper in the 1950s, under the leadership of Pierre Martineau, sponsored what was probably the largest and most diverse marketing and advertising research staff ever for an advertising medium.

About 1918, the now famous husband-wife team of Percival White and Pauline Arnold started the Market Research Co., which later, under the ownership of Samuel Barton, became known as the Market Research Corp. of America (MRCA).

Some of the more familiar pioneer names in research started to flourish in the 1920s. Dr. Daniel Starch, for instance, first used the recognition method for measuring the readership of advertisements and editorial content in magazines and newspapers in 1922.

■ Dr. George Gallup also got into advertising readership measurements in 1923, but he is probably best known today for the Gallup Poll, which was first published in 35 newspapers in 1935 and promptly got him denounced as a "charlatan," a fate that also befell such other pioneer pollsters as Elmo Roper and Archibald Crossley.

These men had a common problem: Convincing skeptical editors and commercial clients that, indeed, a small sample of the population, if properly drawn, could be used to measure accurately the predilections of society. Led by Dr. Gallup in 1936, they turned to public elections; here was a chance to measure just before a public event where real, tabulated results could be compared with survey predictions. Even with the progress since, sampling methodology today still remains the most baffling mystique associated with marketing research.

A young man by the name of Arthur C. Nielsen entered the marketing research field in 1922. He, in effect, invented the concept of share-of-market, which has held business men spellbound ever since; they've spent more to get at that than for anything else in the marketing information field. Result: The A. C. Nielsen Co. is today by far the largest marketing research operation in the world.

The 1930s saw an explosion of new companies dedicated to this new thing called "research." Daniel Starch & Staff (now Starch INRA Hooper Inc.) opened its doors in 1932. Also in that period came Lloyd Hall & Associates, C. E. Hooper Inc., Crossley Inc., Stewart, Dougall & Associates, Elmo Roper & Associates, Psychological Corp., Opinion Research Corp., Willmark Research Corp., and the American Institute of Public Opinion.

Research was starting to become an American export. Dr. George Gallup set up affiliate relationships with survey companies in England and France in 1936,

GEORGE GALLUP　　　**DANIEL STARCH**　　　**ARTHUR NIELSEN**

and A. C. Nielsen started a subsidiary in England in 1939, when World War II started.

War needs spurred the further development of the fledgling research field. Paul Lazarsfeld, the social research scholar, has stressed: "During WW II, social research was in heavy demand by all branches of the government—and especially the Army, the Office of Price Administration and the Office of War Information (OWI)." Much of the OWI work, Mr. Lazarsfeld noted, was done by contract through the Department of Agriculture, where a young psychologist named Rensis Lickert headed the division of program studies. Social scientists were, more and more, drawn into public opinion and attitude research.

After the war, Mr. Lickert took his team to the University of Michigan to create the now-famous Survey Research Center. His counterpart at OWI, research director Elmo Wilson, started his own company, International Research Associates, after the war.

There was a postwar boom in research (as noted in the March 15, 1976, ADVERTISING AGE). Of the Top Ten research companies in the U.S. today, all but one (Nielsen) were founded after WW II. This period also saw the advent of the electronic computer, which broke open the way to large-scale data manipulation.

This brief history, unfortunately, leaves unmentioned many of the prominent shapers of the research community in the U.S. today, and many of the landmark texts, events and contributions that have enriched the field. Nevertheless, it seems evident that marketing and advertising research are more inextricably involved in our country's history than most would guess, except for a backward look prompted by a Bicentennial. #

170 years quelling housewife resistance via ads

Among the big early users of advertising in the nation were the soap companies. The chairman/president of Colgate-Palmolive Co. tells how it was in the beginnings of the Colgate Co., which is celebrating its 170th anniversary.

BY DAVID R. FOSTER
Chairman-President, Colgate-Palmolive Co., New York

Robert Colgate, arriving from England in 1795 to take title to a farm, when title was found to be defective, went into partnership with Ralph Mather in the manufacture of candles and soap in the year 1800. After two years, he dissolved the partnership with Mr. Mather and leased another farm in northern New York.

In 1802, his son, William, financed by his aunt, went into the business of soap manufacture for himself under his own name. The Baltimore venture lasted for young William only a year; he disposed of his business and headed for New York City. After three years of working for a soap and candle maker, he once again set out on his own and settled at 6 Dutch St.

1806 was the start of the business in

First full-color ad for Colgate was this page in McCall's in 1910.

These comments are adapted from a speech given last year to the Newcomen Society. Copyright 1975 by David R. Foster. Reprinted by permission.

his own name—the official founding of the Colgate Co. The young soap maker found that his greatest competitor was the very person whom he hoped would become his best customer; namely, the housewife. The soap of that day was made largely in the home from fats saved by the housewife. It was not too efficient, and not too fragrant. This last fact is of great importance, because the introduction of fragrant flavors into soaps changed the business in a tremendous way. He had to persuade the housewife that his soap was better, cheaper and had a pleasant aroma.

He started to advertise his wares and in 1817 William Colgate placed the following advertisement in a newspaper:

SOAP AND CANDLE MANUFACTORY
WILLIAM COLGATE AND COMPANY
No. 6 Dutch Street, Second Door
From the Corner of
John Street, New York
Have for Sale on Best Terms
a Constant Supply of
Soap, Mould and Dipt Candles
of the First Quality
*Orders for Exportation
Executed on the Shortest Notice*
N.B. The Highest Price Given
for Tallow

This twin need for product and advertising is with us today, and a good description for the history of the company would be: "170 YEARS OVERCOMING HOUSEWIFE RESISTANCE THROUGH ADVERTISING"

Those of you who think we are overreaching the mark by quoting housewife resistance should knock on consumers' doors in such diverse places as Fort Wayne, Providence, London, Beirut, Birmingham, Dakar, Belfast, Zurich, Hamburg and Kuala Lumpur. I can assure you that housewife resistance is there to be overcome, one way or another. A new product must show her the advantages to be gained by using it.

The expansion of the Colgate business continued. New buildings were erected at 8 and 10 Dutch St. and buildings were rented on William St. The Colgates were pious and prolific. William Colgate set

aside a goodly portion of his income for religious benefactions. He had three able sons among his 11 children. Robert founded what came in time to be the National Lead Co. James founded the brokerage firm of James B. Colgate & Co. Samuel joined his father in the soap business and spent his spare time collecting pamphlets to trace the history of the Baptist Church. With his brother, James, he erected the Colgate Academy Building in Hamilton, N.Y., and in recognition of their gifts to Madison University the name of that institution was changed to Colgate University.

By 1847, in spite of numerous additions, the business had outgrown its New York location. So it was moved across the Hudson River into Jersey City, to the site which the company occupies today. In 1877 another important milestone was reached. Colgate toothpaste was produced, selling then in jars. In 1890, the company introduced one of the first collapsible tubes for Colgate toothpaste. Samuel Colgate's eldest son, Richard, was president when the company celebrated its 100th anniversary in 1906. The factory was closed for the day and a banquet for the 1,000 employes was given at Grand Central Palace on Lexington Ave. In celebration of the anniversary, Richard gave every employe a $5 gold piece for every completed year of continuous service.

In 1906, when the company celebrated its 100th anniversary, the products included laundry soap, 160 different kinds of toilet soap, 625 varieties of perfumes and 2,000 varieties of other kinds of products . . . one of our cost-of-sales task forces would have a heyday with these stock items today!

The Colgate business flourished. It passed from father to son, generation to generation, and with sound business policies, accent on quality, high standards of production and service, it kept pace with the growth of the nation. In 1908, the five Colgate brothers, then in control of the company, turned a family business for 102 years into a publicly owned corporation under the laws of New Jersey.

Meanwhile, the B. J. Johnson Soap Co. started making soap, candles and cheese in Milwaukee in 1864. Caleb Johnson conceived the idea of Palmolive soap, a soap made entirely from vegetable oils—olive and palm. It started as a floating soap, but in 1909 he saw at the St. Louis Exposition French machinery for making hard-milled soaps. Machinery was brought from France and Palmolive soap became what it is today.

In 1910, when Charles Pearce was sales and advertising manager, he attended a convention of advertisers and heard a speech by Claude Hopkins, the most publicized of all the entrepreneurs of advertising before his death in 1933. Johnson and Pearce went to call on Lord & Thomas, Claude Hopkins' advertising agency. Together they worked out an advertising campaign using national magazines. It would exploit the soothing effect of the palm and olive oils in Palmolive soap.

The campaign would offer coupons, each good for a free cake of soap redeemable over the dealers' counters. It would advertise Palmolive's retail price, 10¢, and sell it through grocers as well as the traditional druggist. Other promotional devices and selective ways of getting people to try new Palmolive soap were added: One was a "post-card-coupon scheme," whereby the dealer was given stamp-addressed post cards. He received 36 coupon-post cards for every gross of Palmolive soap purchased, to send out to his good customers. They, in turn, would come into the store and exchange the coupons for a free tablet of Palmolive soap provided they bought one (an early "buy-one-get-one-free").

Sales of Palmolive soap doubled and redoubled until the business on this one item reached such proportions that it was felt desirable to change the corporate name from the B. J. Johnson Co. to the Palmolive Co. This was done in 1917. In 1923, the Palmolive Co. was reorganized as a Delaware corporation and its headquarters moved to Chicago, to occupy the Palmolive Bldg.

On Jan. 1, 1927, Peet Bros. Co. of Kansas City, merged with the Palmolive Co. Peet Bros. manufactured fine laundry soaps and toilet soap, and their two plants at Kansas City and Berkeley, Cal., are still two of the four plants supplying the U.S. with our products today. The other two present-day plants, Jersey City and Jeffersonville, Ind., were Colgate plants and so the merger in 1928 of the Palmolive-Peet Co. and Colgate & Co. gave us the geographical spread of plant and warehouse to economically cover the entire U.S.

We have built no new U.S. soap plants since those early days. Elimination of laundry soap production and its framing operations, high-speed toilet soap lines and compact driers, vertical detergent spray towers operating at high speeds versus slower soap powder equipment,

"Held in high esteem" is what Colgate said of its Violet Toilet Water in an 1878 ad (left). Ad styles changed considerably in the years that followed.

has allowed us to remain in relatively the same acreage in plant since the 1929 merger.

When the two companies merged, Colgate had annual sales of $42,000,000 on which it made net profits of $2,400,000. Palmolive-Peet had sales of $51,000,000 with net profits of a little over $5,000,000. A look at Procter & Gamble at that time shows sales of $156,000,000 or 68% larger than the new Colgate-Palmolive-Peet Co. Last year, P&G, with sales of $4.9 billion, was 88% larger than Colgate at $2.6 billion. However, from 1928 until 1960 Colgate only made two small acquisitions, Kirkman Bros. and Kay Daumit (Lustre-Creme shampoo), whereas in this era P&G made mergers to complement its conventional business (Duz, Spic & Span, American Family), moved into food (Duncan Hines, Big Top and Shortening) and into paper (Charmin). Colgate was, in fact, divesting itself of other U.S. in-

terests. The Delawanna Co., making essential oils and synthetics, was sold in 1928. So was the Troco Co., a subsidiary of Palmolive-Peet, making nut margarine. The edible oil department, refining oil into edible products, in Portland and Kansas City, was disbanded and the land and plant were sold.

However, in the summer of 1929, one year after the merger and two months before the fatal day on Wall St., Charlie Pearce was working on an idea brought to him by the National City Co., banking rival of J. P. Morgan. Why not set up a combine of food and drug companies, both manufacturers and retailers, to carry certain standard products straight from the plant to the consumer? This gargantuan trust, which would easily be the most powerful food corporation in the U.S., would have Colgate-Palmolive-Peet as its nucleus. To such a daring plan Pearce could not say "no." he agreed and set to work.

The first step was to arrange a merger of Colgate with Kraft-Phenix Cheese Corp. valued at $38,000,000 and the Hershey Chocolate Corp. valued at $25,000,-000. This merger, which would combine assets totaling more than $125,000,000, was arranged.

Papers consummating the deal were ready to sign by the end of October. New stock certificates for sale to the public for $50,000,000 of additional capital were being printed. Negotiations with a grocery chain, a meat packer and a canning company had entered preliminary stages. With rumors of the impending combine floating around Wall St., Colgate stock boomed. Up from a low of 63 in May, it touched 90 on Oct. 20, 1929. Nine days later the agreements were signed. Charles Pearce with executives from Kraft, Hershey and the National City Co. went out to lunch to celebrate. The stock market broke that afternoon. The deal hung fire. The option on Hershey expired in January, 1930. The option on Kraft soon afterward. Colgate-Palmolive-Peet stock fell to 40, recovering when the company transferred its listing from the Curb to the Exchange later in the year, then went on falling until eventually it got down to 7. Had the merger of just these three companies taken place, combined sales last year would have been $7.6 billion and it would be the largest consumer products company in the U.S.

■ The Palmolive-Peet management under Charlie Pearce had suffered in the Wall St. crash and now had less than 10% of the common stock; 40% of the voting stock remained in the hands of the Colgate family. Sales had dropped drastically, and Pearce and Felix Lowy, the sales manager, were cutting prices and wheeling and dealing to recover momentum.

In March, 1933, the board met. Charles Pearce was elevated to chairman, and Bayard Colgate, the fourth generation of the family to be in the soap business, was elected president at the age of 35. Felix Lowy and some other of Pearce's management team resigned. The foreign manager, E. H. Little, was recalled from Europe to become vp in charge of sales and advertising. Mr. Little had gone to Europe in 1928.

■ Mergers were made with the Cadum Soap Co. in France and with Binder-Ketels in Germany. Companies were set up in Sweden, Italy, Poland and Switzerland with Mr. Little bringing experienced salesmen from the U.S. to run the new subsidiaries. Helmer Ortengren, Bill Sims, John Elliott and Jerry Straka were just four of these men. In the space of five years, E. H. Little had sown the seeds and formed the structures for Europe that

were to grow lustily after World War II. His acquisitions were made to gain manufacturing facilities for Palmolive soap, not to gain local brands made by these European soap makers. Only Cadum soap, the leading toilet soap in France at the time, was allowed to continue its existence.

Another strategic acquisition was made in 1938 in England. After Munich, management in London felt a war with Hitler

Appearing in England in 1924, this ad was first to use the slogan (appearing here in a subhead) that Colgate still uses in many countries: "Nature's simple rule to keep that schoolgirl complexion."

had only been postponed. Palmolive soap, the leading toilet soap on the British market, was imported from Canada in six gross wooden cases (in fact, these cases served in the early days as filing cabinets at the London office). If war came, it is doubtful if 50,000 gross of soap would get preference each month over vital food and war materials from Canada. So in 1938, Goodwin & Sons, a soap manufacturer in Manchester, was acquired and work was started to get modern soap equipment installed as rapidly as possible.

In October, 1939, one month after the declaration of war, the first tablet of Palmolive soap came off the line in Manchester. One more hurdle had to be cleared —a hurdle put there by our friends at Unilever, who, when soap rationing was imposed, virtually took over the rationing function located at Port Sunlight. Licenses were given on the past year's U.K. production. Goodwins were therefore entitled to a quota on the Brown Windsor and Monogram "G" toilet soap they had manufactured during 1938/1939, about 18% of the total U.K. tonnage. But as Palmolive soap had been imported from Canada there was to be no manufacturing quota for it. Lux would take the market by de-

fault. The case was taken to the House of Commons and it was ruled that the quotas should include soap imported into Britain for local consumption as well as that produced locally.

When the "phony" war erupted into action, things happened fast. One of the first 2,000-lb. German bombs to hit London flattened the Colgate Dental Cream factory there.

Thankfully, it fell on a Sunday morning when no one was at work. Within six months production had started up again in rented premises on Charing Cross Road, which later became the head office of the British company. The RAF quickly retaliated and early in 1941 the Palmolive-Ketels soap works in Hamburg was demolished. About all that was left standing was the tall chimney.

In Britain all production was centered in Manchester after the war. Europe's sales flourished; Palmolive soap was still a leader, and Colgate Dental Cream, shave creams, Ajax cleanser, powdered detergents, liquid cleaners and toilet articles, well advertised and promoted, became leaders in their product fields.

In 1955, a major plant was built in France outside of Paris at Compiegne. Toilet soap is still produced at the old plant at Courbevoie, Paris. Two years later, a plant at Anzio, South of Rome, came on stream.

These four major plants, plus smaller plants in Denmark, Switzerland, Spain, Greece, Belgium, Portugal and Ireland supply products for all countries in Europe. Whereas Palmolive soap was the front-runner before World War II, it was Colgate Dental Cream and powdered detergents that dictated new subsidiaries and new plants in the '50s and '60s. These plants in Malaysia and Thailand were not equipped with any toilet soap-making equipment. Toilet soap in most new countries would be contracted for from local laundry soap makers who would install toilet soap finishing equipment and make Palmolive soap and other company brands to our specifications.

When Mr. G. H. Lesch took over the reins of the company early in 1961, sales were $576,000,000. Of this, $301,000,000 was foreign sales. U.S. domestic sales were down and so were domestic earnings. We were in trouble. Franchises of market leaders like Palmolive soap, Ajax cleanser and Colgate Dental Cream had received severe setbacks, caused by better competitive formulations and some particularly serious blunders on the part of our marketing and advertising people. We had no new products and, if we had, any investment in them would have come straight out of the now-declining profits.

George Lesch set about the task of building a stable of new products. To afford them, and to reverse the earnings trend, cost savings had to be made and task forces were formed to look at every aspect of our business. Risks were weighed and then taken. Formulations sacred for years, were changed. Suppliers were asked to set up joint research programs to seek out new compounds that could cut costs or, more importantly, build new products that would answer new consumer needs. An example was the development of new alkylates and brighteners for cold water washing, the development of a successful new product, Cold Power.

■ New product-investment funds were built from these cost savings, first here in the U.S. and later abroad when it was seen that new products were desperately needed there as well. New product groups, reporting directly to the general manager, were set up in all large and medium-size subsidiaries. New U.S. products like Ultra Brite, Ajax cleaners, Palmolive Liquid, Colgate Dental Cream with MFP, and Cold Power were adapted to foreign markets, and even their advertising went with them. Madge, the manicurist, is extolling the virtues of Palmolive Liquid in four or five languages.

A few small acquisitions were made in the early '60s: Sterno Canned Heat, premoistened towelettes from Canaan Products and Reefer-Galler moth chemicals were acquired to round out the line of products in the associated products division. Lakeside Laboratories was purchased to enter the ethical drug market, but it was too small and too limited in scope to develop successfully. We sold it last year for 30 times earnings. And the Wildroot Co.? Well, that died on our doorstep!

It was obvious, in the '70s, that in the U.S. many of our conventional categories, like toilet soap, toothpaste and detergents were not going to grow much faster than population or new home growth. They had reached an in-home incidence that could not be increased. Also, in these and other conventional categories, we came up against P&G, and there is no denying its marketing and technical ability. We knew we had to grow faster than population growth in the U.S. to achieve our goals. We would still maintain our high level of activity on internally produced new products, but we would look at broadening the base of our customer-oriented business by several well chosen acquisitions.

In 1972, we acquired the Kendall Co. of Boston, a fine $300,000,000 company making hospital products, bandages, nonwoven fabrics, sporting goods, textiles and tape coatings for industrial piping (oil and gas pipelines). It had a strong U.S. position with minor penetration abroad in which we could assist to broaden. That we have done.

In 1973, we acquired Helena Rubinstein, one of the four internationally based U.S. cosmetics houses, with its accent on skin treatment lines. A $100,000,000 company with problems in the home market which we have gone a long way to rectify already. Our next objective was to get into the participant sports field, just as Kendall, with subsidiaries in Southern Athletic, Nelson Knitting, Bike and Victoriaville Hockey Sticks took us into team sports. We started with golf and acquired Craigton, Penfold and Morton-Knight in the United Kingdom to give us a complete range in the United Kingdom and Europe. Next we looked in the United States market, and RAM became our golfing partner here. Tennis was the next obvious consumer sport to enter, and last year we reached agreement with the Bancroft Racquet Co. #

That oldtime packaging: Tins, sacks and barrels

BY FRANCIS MAIR
Senior Associate & Museum Dir.
Landor Associates, San Francisco

The evolution of packaging in the U.S. is a broad, curious and complicated story closely entwined with great socio-economic forces and change. Thousands of old packages bear witness to that story at the Landor Associates Museum of Packaging Antiquities in San Francisco.

At the time of the American Revolution, the population of the colonies was considerably less than 4,000,000 people, most of them living in rural communities. Since farmers were basically self-suffi-cient and grew their own food, except for certain staples, individual packaging was of no great importance. The most common forms of packaging in use at that time were bags, glass, crockery, tinware and wood. Generally, these packages contained bulk quantities. In addition, the packages were largely hand-made.

Soon after 1800, two inexorable historical forces caused a change toward packaging as we know it today. These were the Industrial Revolution and the resultant immigration to the cities by agrarian people. On the farm there was adequate storage for a goodly supply of food that needed to be preserved, cured or dried. In the towns and cities, however, this was not the case. Less storage area meant more frequent purchases in smaller amounts. This buying trend led to smaller, individual packages.

Some ascribe the development of the individual portion package to the Shakers. They packaged their seed and herbs in small paper envelopes. Naturally, there were many other products that were packaged in individual portions: Spirits, medicines, tobacco and cosmetics. The first two items were usually contained in glass, although pills were often sold in tins during the 19th century—even as aspirin is today. Tobacco was packaged in tin and cloth, cigars in wood; and cosmetics were commonly available in metal and glass containers.

Paper is perhaps the most economical packaging material. It has been around a long time. Again, need and the Industrial Revolution led to the production of cheap paper. The first machine which mass-produced paper was developed by the Fourdrinier brothers in France and England and first installed in the U.S. in Columbia County, New York, in 1827.

■ The importance of this machine to packaging is inestimable for it made possible the production of many paper products on a large scale, including paperboard, labels and paper bags. While the paper bag concept has been around for a long time, these were first manufactured and sold in the U.S. during the mid-1800s. Their role in supermarkets, department and drugstores as convenience packages for the customers, as well as advertising vehicles, has been well established in this country. Paper sacks are

Old bottles include (l. to r.) a late 1800s candy bottle wtih tragedy and comedy masks, a Chestnut Grove whisky bottle of about 1850 that came West as a water bottle, and a log cabin version for bitters, a patented medicine that was a more acceptable way to imbibe alcohol.

Shape was the thing long ago

Log cabin motif was big in the 1920s. Towle's Log Cabin syrup was one of many tin containers.

also vital to the flour and sugar industries, probably following the original pattern of the cloth sack.

When paperboard became popular, because of mass production in the late 1860s, many new types of products were packaged, including items of wearing apparel, hat pins and sewing equipment. Items in paperboard for service industries, such as spark plugs, fan belts and hardware did not become realities until the 20th century. However, the first use of paperboard for the packaging of food was by Uneeda-National Biscuit around 1890. A general trend of replacing bulk cloth sacks, which contained foodstuffs like flour, potatoes, onions and sugar, with paper sacks then entered the packaging scene.

■ Changes in technology and life style in the early 20th century were reflected in more changes in packaging. Bulk packaging was common in the local general store. And these "Mom and Pop" stores were originally located near stage stops—and later, near railroad stations. The customer wanted one-stop shopping and the general store provided a wide variety of merchandise, albeit a small selection. The automobile changed all that, making possible longer trips to nearby cities for a greater variety in shopping. The general store in small communities was doomed. With mass production came the convenience package.

Corrugated board was first developed in 1856, but the machinery to produce it

In the 1920s, a Coca-Cola barrel of Coke syrup carried a label, "prepared from coca leaves (cocaine removed). Caffeine substituted.

didn't follow until 1871, invented by Robert Gair. However, it took almost 50 years before the railroads would accept it for shipping over the bulkier and heavier wooden boxes. Today, the ubiquitous production of corrugated board runs into

hundreds of different types for specific purposes.

The tin can came about as a British extension of sterilized canning of food for Napolean's armies. The tin can got to the U.S. in 1819. Tin cans were produced by numerous small shops which eventually combined to form the giant can companies. Today cans can be turned out at the amazing rate of 1,200 per minute on a single machine. In the last several years, self-opening closures for liquid products in cans have proliferated due to their increased convenience. Cans have become lighter and lighter in weight resulting in improved freight costs.

■ The greatest revolution in packaging of the early years of this century was the invention by Owens of the automatic bottle blowing machine. In the 18th century bottles were completely handblown. In the 19th century, they were handblown into molds and were, consequently, much more uniform—but still not perfect. The Owens machine changed that and ushered in the era of glass packages that now came off the blowing by billions each year. Uniform openings manufactured by the Owens process, and subsequent machines, have made possible a vast variety of effective closing devices on bottles.

Film Since the '20s

The next striking development in packaging, which occured in the early 20th century, was the use of film. Flexible,

Forerunner of the Kleenex box, this elaborate paperboard container—the Dinkelspiel box—for ladies' hankerchiefs dates back to 1870.

The revolution in packaging was sparked by Uneeda-National Biscuit Co. about 1890, when it launched the first paperboard box of crackers—but it was a front-runner in cracker tins, too.

A small cloth sack for tobacco was ostensibly for Civil War soldiers, circa 1860-64.

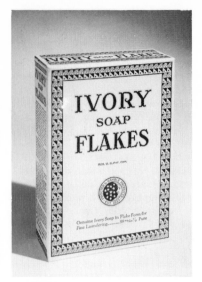

A classic package of Procter & Gamble's Ivory soap flakes in the 1920s still looks good today.

transparent and ultimately heat-sealable, its impact on packaging has been profound. Sophisticated variations in film packaging have made this medium a continuing innovation in package design. DuPont acquired the American rights to cellophane in 1923. Yet this film was not moisture proof. But three years later the problem was solved and another revolution in packaging was on the way.

Baking products, like bread, had been wrapped in wax paper before film took over. Printing on film, as it has been done on other materials, was largely by flexography—rubber printing plates. The reproduction is comparatively coarse, but the impact on the consumer is there. Over the years, subsequent refinements in printing on film have been made, and the character of glass-transparency has been a strong point in favor of film usage for products where the package must be flexible.

Sturdier films have produced the blister packs, largely vacuum formed or blistered over the contained product on a paperboard backing. The versatility of film has resulted in a vast proliferation of chemically engineered package materials suited to particular product requirements. Laminations with other materials for strength and other characteristics have broadened the kinds and qualities of packages in many areas.

Aluminum Changes All

Since World War II, aluminum has become a major factor in packaging. First as a laminate of foil on paper and paperboard, and then as the lids of cans, followed by the total can of aluminum—totally recyclable. Aluminum's value as a packaging medium centers largely around its reflectivity, which attracts attention, and its function as a moisture barrier. There have been many other combinations and applications, such as foil and film.

■ Blown plastic containers in PVC, polystyrene, polyethylene, etc., have made substantial changes in the last decade in the packaging of many products formerly contained in glass. These include bleaches, detergents, chemicals, pharmaceuticals and drugs. Food has been slow to appear in blown plastic because of government regulations requiring the inertness and non-contamination of product in food-container packages. Furthermore, the quality of transparency has been a problem. Feverish research activity is now taking place to develop blown plastic packaging, particularly for beer and soft drinks.

Another innovation, foamed plastic, has recently assumed a role in the packaging picture for the protection of more expensive products. The current thrust in packaging is toward lighter, thinner, more transparent packages specifically created to achieve marketing and merchandising goals.

Drug tins from Parke, Davis & Co. in 1910 were for use in drugstores.

The rhetoric of democracy

Daniel Boorstin is Librarian of Congress, a Rhodes scholar, lawyer, musician and historian, and is the author of "The Americans: The Colonial Experience," which won the Bancroft Award in 1959; "The Lost World of Thomas Jefferson" and other works.

BY DANIEL J. BOORSTIN

Advertising, of course, has been part of the mainstream of American civilization, although you might not know it if you read the most respectable surveys of American history. It has been one of the enticements to the settlement of this New World, it has been a producer of the peopling of the United States, and in its modern form, in its worldwide reach, it has been one of our most characteristic products.

Never was there a more outrageous or more unscrupulous or more ill-informed advertising campaign than that by which the promoters for the American colonies brought settlers here. Brochures published in England in the 17th century, some even earlier, were full of hopeful overstatements, half-truths and downright lies, along with some facts which nowadays surely would be the basis for a restraining order from the Federal Trade Commission. Gold and silver, fountains of youth, plenty of fish, venison without limit, all these were promised, and, of course, some of them were found. It would be interesting to speculate on how long it might have taken to settle this continent if there had not been such promotion by enterprising advertisers. How has American civilization been shaped by the fact that there was a kind of natural selection here of those people who were willing to believe advertising?

U.S. Slogan: 'A New Order'

Advertising has taken the lead in promising and exploiting the new. This was a new world, and one of the advertisements for it appears on the dollar bill

on the Great Seal of the United States, which reads *novus ordo seclorum,* one of the most effective advertising slogans to come out of this country. "A new order of the centuries"—belief in novelty and in the desirability of opening novelty to everybody has been important in our lives throughout our history and especially in this century. Again and again advertising has been an agency for inducing Americans to try anything and everything—from the continent itself to a new brand of soap. As one of the more literate and poetic of the advertising copywriters, James Kenneth Frazier, a Cornell graduate, wrote in 1900 in "The Doctor's Lament":

This lean M.D. is Dr. Brown
Who fares but ill in Spotless Town.
The town is so confounded clean,
It is no wonder he is lean,
He's lost all patients now, you know,
Because they use *Sapolio.*

The same literary talent that once was used to retail Sapolio was later used to induce people to try the Edsel or the Mustang, to experiment with Lifebuoy or Body-All, to drink Pepsi-Cola or Royal Crown Cola, or to shave with a Trac II razor.

And as expansion and novelty have become essential to our economy, advertising has played an ever larger role: In the settling of the continent, in the expansion of the economy, and in the building of an American standard of living. Advertising has expressed the optimism, the hyperbole, and the sense of community, the sense of reaching which has been so important a feature of our civilization.

The Significance of Advertising

Here I wish to explore the significance of advertising, not as a force in the economy or in shaping an American standard of living, but rather as a touchstone of the ways in which we Americans have learned about all sorts of things.

The problems of advertising are, of course, not peculiar to advertising, for they are just one aspect of the problems of democracy. They reflect the rise of what I have called Consumption Communities and Statistical Communities, and many of the special problems of adver-

tising have arisen from our continuously energetic effort to give everybody everything.

If we consider democracy not just as a political system, but as a set of institutions which do aim to make everything available to everybody, it would not be an overstatement to describe advertising as the characteristic rhetoric of democracy. One of the tendencies of democracy, which Plato and other antidemocrats warned against a long time ago, was the danger that rhetoric would displace or at least overshadow epistemology; that is, *the temptation to allow the problem of persuasion to overshadow the problem of knowledge.*

Democratic societies tend to become more concerned with what people believe than with what is true, to become more concerned with credibility than with truth. All these problems become accentuated in a large-scale democracy like ours, which possesses all the apparatus of modern industry. And the problems are accentuated still further by universal literacy, by instantaneous communication, and by the daily plague of words and images.

How the Term Developed

In the early days it was common for advertising men to define advertisements as a kind of news. The best admen, like the best journalists, were supposed to be those who were able to make their news the most interesting and readable. This was natural enough, since the verb to "advertise" originally meant, intransitively, to take note or to consider. For a person to "advertise" meant originally, in the 14th and 15th centuries, to reflect on something, to think about something. Then it came to mean, transitively, to call the attention of another to something, to give him notice, admonish, warn or inform in a formal or impressive manner. And then, by the 16th century, it came to mean: To give notice of anything, to make generally known. It was not until the late 18th century that the word "advertising" in English came to have a specifically "advertising" connotation as we might say today, and not until the late 19th century that it began to have a specifically commercial connotation.

By 1879 someone was saying, "Don't advertise unless you have something worth advertising." But even into the present century, newspapers continue to call themselves by the title "Advertiser" —for example, the *Boston Daily Advertiser,* which was a newspaper of long tradition and one of the most dignified papers in Boston until William Randolph Hearst took it over in 1917. Newspapers carried "Advertiser" on their mastheads, not because they sold advertisements, but because they brought news.

Now, the main role of advertising in American civilization came increasingly to be that of persuading and appealing rather than that of educating and informing. By 1921, for instance, one of the more popular textbooks, Blanchard's "Essentials of Advertising," began: "Anything employed to influence people favorably is advertising. The mission of advertising is to persuade men and women to act in a way that will be of advantage to the advertiser." This development—in a country where a shared, a rising, and a democratized standard of living was the national pride and the national hallmark—meant that advertising had become the rhetoric of democracy.

What, then, were some of the main features of modern American advertising —if we consider it as a form of rhetoric? First, and perhaps most obvious, is *repetition.* It is hard for us to realize that the use of repetition in advertising is not an ancient device, but a modern one, which actually did not come into common use in American journalism until just past the middle of the 19th century.

Prosaic Content, Ingenious Form

The development of what came to be called "iteration copy" was a result of a struggle by a courageous man of letters and advertising pioneer, Robert Bonner, who bought the old *New York Merchant's Ledger* in 1851 and turned it into a popular journal. He then had the temerity to try to change the ways of James Gordon Bennett, who of course was one of the most successful of the American newspaper pioneers, and who was both a sensationalist and at the same time an extremely stuffy man when it came to things that he did not consider to be news. Bonner was determined to use advertisements in Bennett's wide-circulating *New York Herald* to sell his own literary product, but he found it difficult to persuade Bennett to allow him to use any but agate type in his advertising. (Agate was the smallest type used by newspapers in that day, only barely legible to the naked eye.) Bennett would not allow advertisers to use larger type, nor would he allow them to use illustrations except stock cuts, because he thought it was undigni-

Benjamin Franklin's Pennsylvania Gazette was considered the liveliest newspaper of its colonial period and it also had the biggest circulation and advertising revenue.

fied. He said, too, that to allow a variation in the format of ads would be undemocratic. He insisted that all advertisers use the same size type so that no one would be allowed to prevail over another simply by presenting his message in a larger, more clever, or more attention-getting form.

Finally Bonner managed to overcome Bennett's rigidity by leasing whole pages of the paper and using the tiny agate type to form larger letters across the top of the page. In this way he produced a message such as "Bring home the *New York Ledger* tonight." His were unimaginative

messages, and when repeated all across the page they technically did not violate Bennett's agate rule. But they opened a new era and presaged a new freedom for advertisers in their use of the newspaper page. Iteration copy—the practice of presenting prosaic content in ingenious, repetitive form—became common, and nowadays of course is commonplace.

A second characteristic of American advertising which is not unrelated to this is the development of *an advertising style.* We have histories of most other kinds of style—including the style of many unread writers who are remembered today only because they have been forgotten—but we have very few accounts of the history of advertising style, which of course is one of the most important forms of our language and one of the most widely influential.

The development of advertising style was the convergence of several very respectable American traditions. One of these was the tradition of the "plain style," which the Puritans made so much of and which accounts for so much of the strength of the Puritan literature. The "plain style" was of course much influenced by the Bible and found its way into the rhetoric of American writers and speakers of great power like Abraham Lincoln. When advertising began to be self conscious in the early years of this century, the pioneers urged copywriters not to be too clever, and especially not to be fancy.

One of the pioneers of the advertising copywriters, John Powers, said, for example, "The commonplace is the proper level for writing in business; where the first virtue is plainness, 'fine writing' is not only intellectual, it is offensive." George P. Rowell, another advertising pioneer, said, "You must write your advertisement to catch damned fools—not college professors." He was a very tactful person. And he added, "And you'll catch just as many college professors as you will of any other sort."

In the 1920s, when advertising was beginning to come into its own, Claude Hopkins, whose name is known to all in the trade, said, "Brilliant writing has no place in advertising. A unique style takes attention from the subject. Any apparent effort to sell creates corresponding resistance . . . One should be natural and simple. His language should not be conspicuous. In fishing for buyers, as in fishing for bass, one should not reveal the hook." So there developed a characteristic advertising style in which plainness, the phrase that anyone could understand, was a distinguishing mark.

Ads: Davy Crockett and 99.44% Pure

At the same time, the American advertising style drew on another, and what might seem an antithetic, tradition—the tradition of hyperbole and talk, talk, the language of Davy Crockett and Mike Fink. While advertising could think of itself as 99.44% pure, it used the language of "Toronado" and "Cutlass." As I listen to the radio in Washington, I hear a celebration of heroic qualities which would make the characteristics of Mike Fink and Davy Crockett pale, only to discover at the end of the paean that what I have been hearing is a description of the Ford dealers in the District of Columbia neighborhood. And along with the folk tradition of hyperbole and tall talk comes the

rhythm of folk music. We hear that Pepsi-Cola hits the spot, that it's for the young generation—and we hear other products celebrated in music which we cannot forget and sometimes don't want to remember.

There grew somehow out of all these contradictory tendencies—combining the commonsense language of the "plain style," and the fantasy language of "tall talk"—an advertising style. This characteristic way of talking about things was especially designed to reach and catch the millions. It created a whole new world of myth. A myth, the dictionary tells us, is a notion based more on tradition or convenience than on facts; it is a received

idea. Myth is not just fantasy and not just fact, but exists in a limbo, in the world of the "Will to Believe," which William James has written about so eloquently and so perceptively. This is the world of the neither true nor false—of the statement that 60% of the physicians who expressed a choice said that our brand of aspirin would be more effective in curing a simple headache than any other leading brand.

That kind of statement exists in a penumbra. I would call this the "advertising penumbra." It is not untrue, and yet, in its connotation it is not exactly true.

■ Now, there is still another characteris-

HIS MASTER'S VOICE

Four Million Dollars' Worth

of Victor Talking Machines and Records were sold last year. This is one-fifth of the whole amount paid for amusements in all the theatres in the United States. Why don't you get a *Victor* and have theatre and opera in your own home? The *Victor* is easy to play, and *Victor* Records will stand rough handling —children can use them and enjoy them as much as grown folks.

THE VICTOR TALKING MACHINE

won the Gold Medal over all other talking machines at Buffalo. It was awarded by eight distinguished judges—confirmed by three more; confirmed again by a final one—a unanimous verdict of superiority by twelve distinguished men. What they found out is exactly what you want to know. They judged it for you. This alone is decisive, but this is not all. The *Victor* is sent on approval. You judge it yourself. Your money back if you want it. **Sousa**, the March King, says: "The Victor Talking Machine is all right."

Distributing Agents for the Victor Talking Machine

CHICAGO, ILL.—The Talking Machine Co., 107 Madison St.
CHICAGO, ILL.—Lyon & Healy.
NEW YORK, N.Y.—Victor Distributing & Export Company, No. 1 Broadway.
NEW YORK, N.Y.—C. Bruno & Son, 350 Broadway.
SYRACUSE, N.Y.—W. D. Andrews.
BOSTON, Mass.—The Eastern Talking Machine Co.
KANSAS CITY, Mo.—J. F. Schmelzer & Sons Arms Co.
EVANSVILLE, IND.—L. K. Ashby Bicycle Co.

DALLAS, TEXAS—Singer Bros. Dry Goods Co.
JACKSONVILLE, FLA.—Metropolitan Talking Machine Co.
PHILADELPHIA, PA.—Western Electric Co., 933 Market St.
NEW ORLEANS, LA.—National Automatic Fire Alarm Co.
CINCINNATI, Ohio—The Rudolph Wurlitzer Co.
BALTIMORE, Md.—H. R. Eisenbrandt's Sons.
BUFFALO, N.Y.—P. A. Powers, 643 Main St.
ST. LOUIS, Mo.—Simmons Hardware Co.

ST. LOUIS, Mo.—Victor Talking Machine, Limited, Carleton Building.
SAN FRANCISCO, CAL.—Sherman Clay & Co.
ST. PAUL, MINN.—Koehler & Hinrichs.
LINCOLN, NEB.—The Wittmann Co.
OMAHA, NEB.—A. Hospe, Jr.
PITTSBURGH, PA.—S. Hamilton.
DETROIT, Mich.—Grinnell Brothers.
INDIANAPOLIS, IND.—Carlin & Lennox.

Victor Talking Machine Co., Stephen Girard Bldg., Philadelphia

Since early in this century, the familiar Victor symbol has been around, later under the RCA-Victor name. English painter Francis Barroud spotted his dog, Nipper, listening to voices in the horn, used what he saw and a famous trademark then was born.

tic of advertising so obvious that we are inclined perhaps to overlook it. I call that *ubiquity*. Advertising abhors a vacuum and we discover new vacuums every day. The parable, of course, is the story of the man who thought of putting the advertisement on the other side of the cigaret package. Until then, that was wasted space, and a society which aims at a democratic standard of living, at extending the benefits of consumption and all sorts of things and services to everybody, must miss no chances to reach people. The highway billboard and other outdoor advertising, bus and streetcar and subway advertising, and skywriting, radio and tv commercials—all these are of course obvious evidence that advertising abhors a vacuum.

We might reverse the old mousetrap slogan and say that anyone who can devise another place to put another mousetrap to catch a consumer will find people beating a path to his door. "Avoiding advertising will become a little harder next January," the *Wall Street Journal* reported on May 17, 1973, "when a Studio City, Cal., company launches a venture called StoreVision. Its product is a system of billboards that move on a track across supermarket ceilings. Some 650 supermarkets so far are set to have the system." All of which helps us understand the observation attributed to a French man of letters during his recent visit to Times Square. "What a beautiful place, if only one could not read!"

Bumper Sticker to Airplane Streamer

Everywhere is a place to be filled, as we discover in a recent *Publishers Weekly* description of one advertising program:

"The $1.95 paperback edition of Dr. Thomas A. Harris' million-copy best seller, 'I'm O.K., You're O.K.' is in for full-scale promotion in July by its publisher, Ayon Books. Plans range from bumper stickers to airplane streamers, from planes flying above Fire Island, the Hamptons and Malibu. In addition, the $100,000 promotion budget calls for 200,000 bookmarks, plus brochures, buttons, lipcards, floor and counter displays, and advertising in magazines and tv."

The ubiquity of advertising is of course just another effect of our uninhibited efforts to use all the media to get all sorts of information to everybody everywhere. Since the places to be filled are everywhere, the amount of advertising is not determined by the needs of advertising, but by the *opportunities* for advertising which become unlimited.

But the most effective advertising, in an energetic, novelty-ridden society like ours, tends to be "self liquidating." To create a cliché, you must offer something which everybody accepts. The most successful advertising therefore self destructs because it becomes cliché. Examples of this are found in the tendency for copyrighted names of trademarks to enter the vernacular—for the proper names of products which have been made familiar by costly advertising to become common nouns, and so to apply to anybody's products. Kodak becomes a synonym for camera, Kleenex a synonym for facial tissue, when both begin with a small k, and Xerox (now, too, with a small x) is used to describe all processes of copying, and so on.

These are prototypes of the problem. If you are successful enough, then you will defeat your purpose in the long run—by making the name and the message so familiar that people won't notice them, and then people will cease to distinguish your product from everybody else's.

In a sense of course, as we will see, the whole of American civilization is an example. When this was a "new" world, if people succeeded in building a civilization here, the New World would survive and would reach the time—in our age—when it would cease to be new. And now we have the oldest written Constitution in use in the world. This is only a parable, of which there are many more examples.

'Erasure' Assigned to Advertising

The advertising man who is successful in marketing any particular product, then—in our high-technology, well-to-do democratic society, which aims to get everything to everybody—is apt to be diluting the demand for his particular product in the very act of satisfying it. But luckily for him, he is at the very same time creating a fresh demand for his services as advertiser.

And as a consequence, there is yet another role which is assigned to American advertising. This is what I call "erasure." Insofar as advertising is competitive or innovation is widespread, erasure is required in order to persuade consumers that this year's model is superior to last year's.

In fact, we consumers learn that we might be risking our lives if we go out on the highway with those very devices that were last year's lifesavers, but without whatever special kind of brakes or wipers or seat belt is on this year's model. This is what I mean by "erasure"—and we see

---

In U.S. Bicentennial, let's help make the difference

Caught up in today's troubles, there's a temptation to evoke ever more rosy images of the 200 years which have preceded this, our nation's Bicentennial year. And coupled with it, too often, a pronounced resignation to a sense of futility, an "I can't-do-anything-about-it feeling."

Overlooked, except in dusty history books, is the evidence that, sometimes, even a single individual has great impact on his times, and can and does help *make the difference*—on company and country.

During George Washington's Presidency (which began in 1789) as today, "inflation and postwar depression strained public purse, temper and credulity," and almost foundered this nation of ours. He helped *make the difference*.

Just one life span later, it took the lives of one of every five of military age to erase slavery from our country. Again

the nation was almost shattered. And again one man really helped *make the difference*, and had great impact on his time and on history.

That man's achievements for his nation, and in overcoming his tribulations, should encourage and inspire us all. For example:

He failed in business	'31
Defeated for legislature	'32
Again failed in business	'33
Elected to legislature	'34
Sweetheart died	'35
Had nervous breakdown	'36
Defeated for Speaker	'38
Defeated for Elector	'40
Defeated for Congress	'43
Elected for Congress	'46
Defeated for Congress	'48
Defeated for Senate	'55

Defeated for Vice-President	'56
Defeated for Senate	'58
Elected President	'60

He never admitted defeat.
His name: Abraham Lincoln.

As our contribution to our nation's Bicentennial, in these betroubled days, let's each of us seek to be part of the solution instead of just part of the problem. Let us remember, always, that in a free society like ours, all of us are responsible for this, our own nation's welfare.

■ Because it's better to light one candle than to curse the darkness, let's try to help *make the difference*.

Sam Krupnick,

Krupnick & Associates, St. Louis, in a letter to clients and friends.

it on our advertising pages or our television screen every day. We read in the *New York Times* (May 20, 1973), for example, that "For the price of something small and ugly, you can drive something small and beautiful"—an advertisement for the Fiat 250 Spider.

Or another, perhaps more subtle example is the advertisment for shirts under a picture of Oliver Drab: "Oliver Drab. A name to remember in fine designer shirts? No kidding . . . Because you pay extra money for Oliver Drab. And for all the other superstars of the fashion world. Golden Vee [the name of the brand that is advertised] does not have a designer's label. But we do have designers . . . By keeping their names *off* our label and simply saying Golden Vee, we can afford to sell our $7-to-$12 shirts for just $7 to $12, which should make Golden Vee a name to remember. Golden Vee, you only pay for the shirt."

Having mentioned two special characteristics—the self-liquidating tendency and the need for erasure—which arise from the dynamism of the American economy, I would like to try to place advertising in a larger perspective. The special role of advertising in our life gives a clue to a pervasive oddity in American civilization. A leading feature of past cultures, as anthropologists have explained, is the tendency to distinguish between "high" culture and "low" culture—between the culture of the literate and the learned on the one hand, and that of the populace on the other. In other words, between the language of literature and the language of the vernacular.

Some of the most useful statements of this distinction have been made by social scientists at the University of Chicago—first by the late Robert Redfield in his several pioneering books on peasant society, and then by Milton Singer in his remarkable study of Indian civilization, "When a Great Tradition Modernizes" (1972). This distinction between the great tradition and the little tradition, between the high culture and the folk culture, has begun to become a commonplace of modern anthropology.

It's Not Chaucer or Shakespeare

Some of the obvious features of advertising in modern America offer us an opportunity to note the significance or insignificance of that distinction for us. Elsewhere I have tried to point out some of the peculiarities of the American attitude toward the *high* culture. There is something distinctive about the place of thought in American life, which I think is not quite what it has been in certain Old World cultures.

But what about distinctive American attitudes to *popular* culture? What is our analog to the folk culture of other peo-

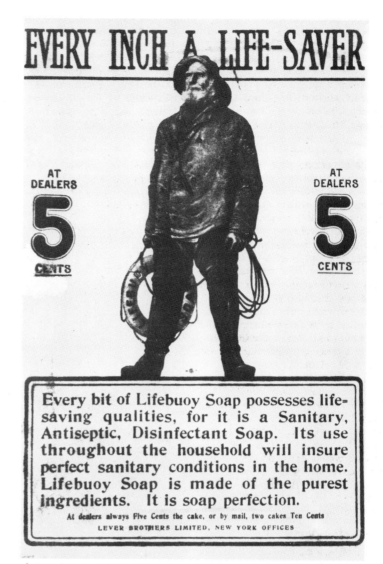

Appearing in 1902, this ad pushed Lever Bros. Lifebuoy soap.

ples? Advertising gives us some clues—to a characteristically American democratic folk culture. Folk culture is a name for the culture which ordinary people everywhere lean on. It is not the writings of Dante and Chaucer and Shakespeare and Milton, the teachings of Machiavelli and Descartes, Locke or Marx. It is, rather, the pattern of slogans, local traditions, tales, songs, dancers and ditties. And of course, holiday observances.

Popular culture in other civilizations has been, for the most part, both an area of continuity with the past, a way in which people reach back into the past and out to their community, and at the same time an area of local variations. An area of individual and amateur expression in which a person has his own way of saying, or notes his mother's way of saying or singing, or his own way of dancing, his own view of folk wisdom and the cliché.

Low Culture Takes Control

And here is an interesting point of contrast. In other societies outside the

United States, it is the *high* culture that has generally been an area of centralized, organized control. In Western Europe, for example, universities and churches have tended to be closely allied to the government. The institutions of higher learning have had a relatively limited access to the people as a whole. This was inevitable, of course, in most parts of the world, because there were so few universities. In England, for example, there were only two universities until the early 19th century. And there was central control over the printed matter that was used in universities or in the liturgy. The government tended to be close to the high culture, and that was easy because the high culture itself was so centralized and because literacy was relatively limited.

In our society, however, we seem to have turned all of this around. Our high culture is one of the least centralized areas of our culture. And our universities express the atomistic, diffused, chaotic, and individualistic aspect of our life. We have in this country more than 2,500 colleges and universities, institutions of so-called higher learning. We have a vast population in these institutions, somewhere over 7,000,000 students.

But when we turn to our popular culture, what do we find? We find that in our nation of Consumption Communities and emphasis on Gross National Product (GNP) and growth rates, advertising has become the heart of the folk culture and even its very prototype. And as we have seen, American advertising shows many characteristics of the folk culture of other societies: Repetition, a plain style, hyperbole and tall talk, folk verse, and folk music. Folk culture, wherever it has flourished, has tended to thrive in a limbo between fact and fantasy, and of course, depending on the spoken word and the oral tradition, it spreads easily and tends to be ubiquitous. These are all familiar characteristics of folk culture and they are ways of describing our folk culture, but how do the expressions of our peculiar folk culture come to *us*?

■ They no longer sprout from the earth, from the village, from the farm, or even from the neighborhood or the city. They come to us primarily from enormous centralized self-consciously *creative* (an overused word, for the overuse of which advertising agencies are in no small part responsible) organizations. They come from advertising agencies, from networks of newspapers, radio, and television, from outdoor-advertising agencies, from the copywriters for ads in the largest-circulation magazines, and so on. These "crea-

tors" of folk culture—or pseudo-folk culture—aim at the widest intelligibility and charm and appeal.

But in the United States, we must recall, the advertising folk culture (like all advertising) is also confronted with the problems of self-liquidation and erasure. These are by-products of the expansive, energetic character of our economy. And they, too, distinguish American folk culture from folk cultures elsewhere.

Our Culture, Like Ads, Is Fleeting

Our folk culture is distinguished from others by being discontinuous, ephemeral, and self-destructive. Where does this leave the common citizen? All of us are qualified to answer.

In our society, then, those who cannot lean on the world of learning, on the high culture of the classics, on the elaborated wisdom of the books, have a new problem. The University of Chicago, for example, in the 1930s and 1940s was the center of a quest for a "common discourse." The champions of that quest, which became a kind of crusade, believed that such a discourse could be found through familiarity with the classics of great literature—and especially of Western European literature. I think they were misled; such works were not, nor are they apt to become, the common discourse of our society. Most people, even in a democracy, and a rich democracy like ours, live in a world of popular culture, our special kind of popular culture.

The characteristic folk culture of our

society is a creature of advertising, and in a sense it *is* advertising. But advertising, our own popular culture, is harder to make into a source of continuity than the received wisdom and common-sense slogans and catchy songs of the vivid vernacular. The popular culture of advertising attenuates and is always dissolving before our very eyes. Among the charms, challenges, and tribulations of modern life, we must count this peculiar fluidity, this ephemeral character of that very kind of culture on which other peoples have been able to lean, the kind of culture to which they have looked for the continuity of their traditions, for their ties with the past and with the future.

No More Individual Expression?

We are perhaps the first people in history to have a centrally organized mass-produced folk culture. Our kind of popular culture is here today and gone tomorrow—or the day after tomorrow. Or whenever the next semi-annual model appears. And insofar as folk culture becomes advertising, and advertising becomes centralized, it becomes a way of depriving people of their opportunities for individual and small-community expression. Our technology and our economy and our democratic ideals have all helped make that possible. Here we have a new test of the problem that is at least as old as Heraclitus—an everyday test of man's ability to find continuity in his experience. And here democratic man has a new opportunity to accommodate himself, if he can, to the unknown. #

Advertising: Stepchild of the First Amendment?

BY FORMER SEN. SAM J. ERVIN JR.

There is no greater bulwark for freedom in our land than that provision in the First Amendment which reads, "Congress shall make no law . . . abridging the freedom of speech, or of the press . . ." Since its adoption in 1791 as part of the Bill of Rights, it has come to distinguish this country from almost every other in the world as a nation whose people are free to express their ideas and opinions without fear of government retaliation. It is the very heart of our system of government which depends upon an informed public and robust political debate. The First Amendment's protection of freedom of speech and freedom of press has given meaning to our traditional respect for the worth of the individual human being, and vitality to our belief in the possibility of mankind's continuing self enlightenment.

■ In the final analysis, what the framers

American public. Increased subpoenaing of newsman, the Justice Department's effort to enjoin publication of the so-called 'Pentagon papers," and expanding of government control and regulation of broadcasting are just a few of the reminders that government cannot be trusted to honor the commandments of the First

Questions about freedom of speech, particularly "commercial speech" (advertising) and its importance, or lack of it, in the American social and economic structure, are raised by Mr. Ervin. From that, the former senator from the tobacco-growing state of North Carolina leads into his objections to rulings, upheld by the U.S. Supreme Court, outlawing tv and radio commercials for cigarets and disallowing tobacco industry replies to anti-smoking accouncements under the "fairness doctrine."

Without necessarily agreeing with all of the former senator's conclusions on cigaret advertising, AA presents his thoughtful analysis as important for its implications (including possible future abridgement of freedom) for advertising in all fields. His comments are excerpted from a talk at the annual meeting of the Proprietary Assn. at White Sulphur Springs, W. Va., and are reprinted from the July 17, 1972, issue of ADVERTISING AGE.

of the First Amendment did was to stake the very existence of America as a free society upon their faith that it has nothing to fear from the exercise of First Amendment freedoms, no matter how much they may be abused, as long as it leaves truth free to combat error.

In recent years, the First Amendment's guarantee of freedom of expression has come under considerable attack. All branches of government, at almost every level, have been tempted to interfere with the gathering, editing, publication, or distribution of information to the

Amendment.

One area of freedom of expression in which the government has become increasingly involved is with respect to commercial advertising. Two separate developments in the interpretation of the First Amendment have opened the doors for the considerable and increasing government regulation of advertising.

In the first instance, the courts have promulgated a theory of the First Amendment which distinguishes between "commercial speech" and other forms of speech, giving greater constitutional pro-

tection to the latter than the former.

The second important development which has led to increasing government regulation of "commercial speech" is the application of the First Amendment to broadcasting in a different manner than to the printed press. Government regulation of broadcasting, especially commercial advertising on the air, has been established by Congress, implemented by the Federal Communications Commission, and sustained by the courts in a manner which would be rejected out of hand as unconstitutional if applied to the printed press.

'Commercial Speech' Less Vital?

In general, the courts have adopted and applied a First Amendment theory distinguishing between "commercial" speech and other speech on the basis of an asserted difference in the social purpose and value of these types of speech. They have determined that "commercial speech" is designed simply to entice consumers to purchase services or products, and that it does not serve the same high social purpose as does speech which advocates a certain political or religious position, presents general information, or involves the dissemination of culturally valuable matter.

In the case of *Valentine v. Christensen*, 316 U.S. 52 (1941), the Supreme Court first set forth explicitly this theory of discriminating against "commercial speech" in applying the First Amendment. This case involved a constitutional challenge to a New York City ordinance prohibiting the distribution of "commercial and business advertising matter" in public places. In dismissing the constitutional objections to the ordinance, the court said:

"This court has unequivocally held that the streets are proper places for the exercise of the freedom of communicating information and disseminating opinion, and that though the states and municipalities may appropriately regulate the privilege in the public interest, they may not unduly burden or proscribe its employment in these public thoroughfares. We are equally clear that the Constitution imposes no such restraint on government as respects purely commercial advertising."

■ The Supreme Court did not then, nor has it since, given us the benefit of the wisdom which underlies such a distinction. It simply asserted that "purely commercial advertising" was an inferior form of expression, a black sheep not embraced by the protective care of the First Amendment. Unfortunately, since this decision, state and federal courts alike have echoed almost in unison the same chorus, again without much explanation. Despite their uniform refrain that "commercial speech" is not entitled to First Amendment protection, they still have not put to rest those few souls who still ask why.

Ads Bring Informed Consumer

The First Amendment was quite clearly adopted to protect the free communication and exchange of ideas. Nowhere in the Constitution is there any explicit limitation of the First Amendment's protection to a particular type of expression.

Private economic decisions made in a free enterprise economy by millions of individual consumers depend upon a wide dissemination of information to the consuming public about the various economic and financial choices available. Our society has an interest in encouraging its consumers to be knowledgeable consumers.

We all know that advertising has been an important source of new ideas about various possibilities of life styles available in our great country. Especially through the medium of television, advertising has brought to millions of Americans new ideas, not only about which

soap to buy, but where to live, for which goals in life to aspire, what jobs to seek, and what to do with their increasing amounts of leisure time. Quite literally, advertising in America has been one of the most significant of all factors in altering our living habits, our social attitudes and our personal expectations. To dismiss advertising as we know it today in America as nothing more than an offer to sell or an offer to buy is not only to ignore its total impact, but it is to forget about our traditional belief in the importance of the communication of ideas —all kinds of ideas—to the advancement of civilization.

One perceptive critic of the court's discriminatory application of the First Amendment to advertising has written, "Advertising is a medium of information and persuasion, providing much of the day-to-day 'education' of the American public, and facilitating the flexible allocation of resources necessary to a free enterprise economy. Neither profit motivation nor desire to influence private economic decisions necessarily distinguishes the peddlar from the preacher, the publisher, or the politician."

Economic Interests Inferior?

Man is not only a political being. He is not only a spiritual being. Man has infinite dimensions to his being. His economic well being, especially in an affluent country such as ours, constitutes a vital part of his life.

Our free enterprise system rests in part on the notion that a man should be just as free in making decisions affecting his economic well being as he is free to assert his political judgment and his re-

ligious convictions. The better educated Americans become with respect to the innumerable possibilities available to them as workers and consumers, the richer our individual and corporate lives will become.

There are legitimate reasons in particular circumstances for treating advertising differently than other forms of expression. In my opinion, rather than accepting the difficult task of delineating these reasons and clarifying these circumstances, the courts have casually accepted the notion that man's interest in his economic well being is constitutionally inferior to his other interests. This approach is not only judicially unsound, but destructive of First Amendment freedoms.

Another and especially serious threat to freedom in advertising is in the area of broadcasting.

Broadcast Freedom Complexities

When they drafted znd ratified the First Amendment, the founding fathers decreed that the freedoms it secures should extend into the future and apply to all activities falling within their scope, even though such activities were never envisaged by them. As a consequence, the First Amendment freedoms embodied in the phrase "freedom of speech or of the press" confer upon those who broadcast information or ideas by radio or television the constitutional right to do so, subject, however, to certain limitations which are not applicable to the press.

Those who wish to operate as radio or television broadcasters are required to apply for licenses to the FCC, which allocates available broadcast frequencies and compels each broadcaster to broadcast on the frequency allotted to it. These requirements are adjudged valid under the First Amendment simply because in the present state of the science, scarcity of broadcast frequencies and unrestricted broadcasting would prevent intelligible communication of information or ideas on the airwaves.

Radio and television broadcasters are subjected by law to the fairness doctrine as authorized by Congress and expounded by the Supreme Court in *Red Lion Broadcasting Co. v. The Federal Communications Commission*, 295 U.S. 367, and other decisions. The avowed purpose of the fairness doctrine is to further the people's right to know the truth by requiring that discussion of public issues be presented on broadcast stations, and that all sides of the issues be given fair coverage.

Marginal Speech

To this end, the fairness doctrine obligates a radio or television station to give

Scale model is of a visitor orientation center created on the grounds of the Washington Monument by Eastman Kodak Co. and National Park Service. Theater, at right, presents continuous showing of a 12-minute film, "Washington the Man," starring Lorne Greene. Film depicts Washington's role in his own era and his continuing influence on the nation's history.

reply time to answer personal attacks and political editorials broadcast by it, and to extend time to a political candidate if it grants time to his opponent. The station must permit the use of its facilities for these purposes without compensation.

In 1968, the court of appeals for the District of Columbia sustained the Federal Communications Commission's decision to aapply the fairness doctrine to cigaret advertising.

In its infamous opinion, the court of appeals relied in part on the theory enunciated in the Valentine case. It noted, "Promoting the sale of a product does not affect the political process, it does not contribute to the exchange of ideas, does not provide information on matters of public importance, and is not, except perhaps for the admen, a form of individual self expression." The court of appeals ultimately dismissed cigaret advertising as "marginal speech."

Fairness Doctrine—for Everyone?

The court then dismissed the contention of the networks that the First Amendment protects broadcasters from government control of content just as it does the printed press. Merely suggesting that broadcasting was "different in kind" from the printed page, the court quickly brushed aside the networks' constitutional objections. It upheld the FCC's application of the fairness doctrine to cigaret advertising which required that any radio or television station which advertised cigarets must make available a substantial amount of time for "counter advertising."

■ Since this 1968 decision, an almost laughable turn of events has occurred. In order to apply the "fairness doctrine," there had to be a determination that the relationship of smoking to health constituted a "controversial issue of public importance" requiring that a licensee present with reasonable fairness both sides of the issue. That determination was made by the FCC and affirmed by the court of appeals. Subsequently and unfortunately, the Congress enacted a ban on all cigaret advertising on radio and television. This is another and particularly outrageous example of the "stepchild" treatment given to broadcasting with respect to First Amendment principles.

Some time after all cigaret advertising was removed from radio and television, and while anti-smoking advertisements were still being put on the air, the tobacco industry requested the FCC to apply the "fairness doctrine" in such a way as to permit them to respond to these anti-smoking commercials. The tobacco companies did not seek to advertise any particular product or to encourage smok-

ing generally. They simply asked that the FCC require licensees to give them an opportunity to respond to the claims that cigaret smoking is bad for one's health.

Is Final Truth in on Cigarets?

In an ironic and incredible decision, the FCC decided that the fairness doctrine could not apply in this case because, only three short years after the Banzhaf case, the relationship between smoking and health was no longer "a controversial issue of public importance." The FCC's holding was affirmed by the court of appeals for the Fourth Circuit and, upon appeal, affirmed in a *per curiam* decision by the Supreme Court. In effect, the FCC and the courts have determined that the final truth has been established with respect to the health hazards of cigaret smoking.

The impact of the government's intervention in the controversy over the relationship between cigaret smoking and health—first, in requiring counter advertising; secondly, in banning cigaret advertising from television and radio, and finally, in refusing to apply the fairness doctrine to the anti-smoking commercials—is worse than confusing. It represents in its total undertaking an effort by government to deny the public the fullest possible discussion of the particular issue involved. It results in anything but fairness. It undermines First Amendment principles.

Subsequent to the application of the fairness doctrine to cigaret advertising, many individuals and groups have petitioned the FCC to apply the doctrine to other advertising. A reading of several FCC decisions on this subject indicated that the commission is having a very difficult time explaining why counter advertising should not be required of broadcast licensees with respect to many other products than cigarets. Perhaps, ironically enough, in trying to apply the fairness doctrine, the commission will discover that there is a public and social value in commercial advertising, and sometimes even a "political question" attached to certain advertising. If so, the courts as well as the FCC will have to reexamine their assumption that "commercial speech" is devoid of content which the First Amendment was written to protect.

Editor's Note: While this book was in process of being printed, the United States Supreme Court issued an important decision upsetting a State of Virginia law which prohibited pharmacists from using price advertising for prescription drugs.

In doing so, the court in large measure agreed with the thesis expounded here by former Senator Ervin. The majority Supreme Court opinion, written by Justice Blackman, said:

"Our question is whether speech which does 'no more than propose a commercial transaction' is so removed from any 'exposition of ideas' and from 'truth, science, morality and the arts in general, in its diffusion of liberal sentiments on the administration of government' that it lacks all protection [under the First Amendment to the Constituion]. Our answer is that it is not."

Early admen learn how things are down on the farm

Farm magazine and farm equipment advertising both played an important role in the early development of U.S. agriculture. The following unusual tale is about one pioneering farm publisher and the Midwest farm tour he organized in 1914 for eastern admen to help educate them to the marketing potential there. The story is told by one who was there, ex-copywriter and account executive Taylor Adams, now 86 and retired.

BY TAYLOR ADAMS

Nikita Khrushchev, visiting the United States in 1959, insisted on being taken out to the vast fertile heartland of the country. He wanted to see for himself those huge farm "factories" he had heard about. Although he could not know that, years after his death, this region would grow millions of bushels of wheat to feed the Soviet people, his peasant wisdom told him that here, in the almost limitless productivity of the rich alluvial soil, lay the strength of America.

Nor did Mr. Khrushchev know that his tour of inspection of the Corn Belt had been anticipated, nearly half a century before, by a group of advertising men from the eastern states. They came out to see the land, to talk with the men and women who farmed it, lived on it and bought the products advertised in the farm papers. They wanted to meet the merchants and devise better ways of merchandising.

■ The sponsor of the trip was E. T. Meredit, of Des Moines, publisher of *Successful Farming,* the regional farm paper whose 600,000 circulation in 1914 blanketed the nine north central states. Mr. Meredith was a man of energy and vision, already a political leader championing the cause of the farmer, soon to become Secretary of Agriculture under Woodrow Wilson and, in 1922, founder of the magazine that became *Better Homes & Gardens.* He felt this to be a good time for eastern business men to learn that there was more to the "West" than wide-open spaces and Indians.

He knew manufacturers were being hurt by the panic of 1914, and he wanted them to see that the people in this part of the country had not suffered as much as other regions. Besides, he could show them his fine new plant and tell them how *Successful Farming* was growing rapidly in size and importance as an advertising medium.

So Mr. Meredith hired a luxurious special train. (Yes, I said train. There were no 747s in those days; Charles Lindbergh wasn't yet eight years old.) The Meredith Special consisted of five brand new Pullman sleeping cars, a diner and an empty baggage car that was speedily converted into a recreational area with card tables for poker, mats for wrestling, a portable mini-piano and other facilities for the diversion of the tired executive on tour.

Mr. Meredith was a strong supporter of Prohibition, but the Volstead Act was still six years away and he could be a tolerant and entertaining host. There was no drought on the Meredith Special as it rolled along the Main Line of the Pennsylvania Railroad on that sunny afternoon of June 6, 1914, bound for Des

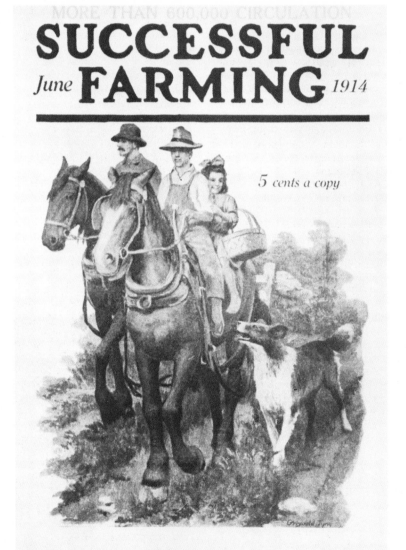

MORE THAN 600,000 CIRCULATION

SUCCESSFUL
June FARMING *1914*

5 cents a copy

WHEN·THE DAY'S WORK IS OVER

When a midwestern farm tour for eastern admen was sprung by publisher E. T. Meredith in 1914, his Successful Farming cover looked like this.

Pulling out the stops, Meredith promoted his "special" with a poster.

Moines with stopovers at farmers' towns in Indiana, Illinois and Iowa. I was there, the only copywriter among nearly three score advertising managers, agency space buyers and executives, publishers' representatives and professors of agronomy and animal husbandry from midwestern colleges.

■ New York's "Big Four" agencies (1913 billings)—Thompson, Batten, Seaman and Presbrey—were well represented. L. H. Ferber and W. H. Meyer came from JWT; from Presbrey, W. A. Baker and Mr. Adams. Frank Lawrence, one of the best-loved media men in the business, signed in from the George Batten Co., along with one-legged H. A. Biggs and Fred Walsh from Frank Seaman Inc., Chesterfield's agency that would spawn Newell-Emmett and today's Cunningham & Walsh. Frank Hermes was there from Blackman, later Blackman-Ross and then Compton Advertising.

H. K. McCann sent vp E. W. Mann. There was small, feisty H. H. Charles, owner of the specialized agricultural advertising service that bore his name; Glenn Flory of Calkins & Holden; Messrs. Dillenbeck and Edwards from Hanff-Metzger; Jack Walsh of Lesan and tenor-voiced Bolton of Perry-Dame—all New Yorkers greeting the men from Boston and the Baltimoreans of Green-Lucas Co. (No, Rubicam wasn't there. Neither were Bill Benton or Chet Bowles, Ted Bates or David Ogilvy. These geniuses were no doubt in summer camp at the time, being taught to swim by crew-cut collegiate counselors.)

When we stopped at Philadelphia to take on that city's contingent, it was noticed that no one from the mighty N. W. Ayer got on—why, I never knew. To atone for this dereliction, there was the legendary A. G. Shew of F. Wallis Armstrong Co., the man who bought 12 four-color pages for Campbell Soup Co., every year in every national magazine, demanding and getting first position. With him was the muscular, red-headed Duncan MacPherson of Ireland Advertising, promptly challenging one and all to wrestle him to the ground. This feat was

accomplished by Fred Walsh right after dinner.

■ Space forbids further nomenclature of the agencies. National advertisers of farmer-bought products were there in force— Exide Storage Batteries, Pittsburgh Steel, American Can, Corn Products, Flintkote, Styleplus Clothes, B. T. Babbitt, Sherwin-Williams, Sharples Cream Separators, Fels-Naphtha, Sweet-Orr and others.

A promotional booklet with this cover told the early farm tour and farm market story for Meredith.

Overnight, the train swung into upper Indiana, beginning a jam-packed, grueling schedule of education, entertainment and getting acquainted. We would pull into some whistle-stop no easterner had ever heard of, to be met by the farmers, often with their wives and children, in big dusty open touring cars and small Tin Lizzies, frequently in horse-drawn wagons. We would be split up into small groups and whizzed off to see the big barns, the tall silos, the tractors, harvestors and new-fangled milking machines.

Joining a group might be the mayor of the town, a member of the local chamber of commerce or a retail storekeeper who would brief us on the bushels-per-acre, the latest price of hogs and corn and beef-on-the-hoof in Chicago. On the one Sunday trip, ministers of five denominations took their respective believers to their local folds. (My parson's text was, "By their fruits ye shall know them"—a statement he amplified with mind-blowing statistics not fully comprehended, I am afraid, by somewhat hung-up city slickers.)

We visited the Iowa State Agricultural College whose president R. A. Pearson lectured us and, with many of his staff, accompanied us for the rest of the tour. We were joined along the way by bankers, business men, publishers and politicians. Among the latter were young Henry Agard Wallace, who was to become FDR's Vice-President, publisher of *Wallace's Farmer*, and Sam McKelvie, owner of the *Nebraska Farmer*, later governor of his state. The tour ended with a banquet and I will spare you the rhetoric of this delightful finale. It had been a good trip; we had made friends and received knowledge and as the strains of "Auld Lang Syne" faded away at midnight, we tottered, bone-weary, to our berths in the now home-directed Meredith Special.

Three weeks later, a fat old archduke was shot by a Serbian terrorist and the world slid into chaos. But armies of millions had to be fed and equipped; the price of wheat skyrocketed, beef cattle reached record highs on the Chicago Exchange, and the Corn Belt burgeoned into prosperity. *Successful Farming's* circulation zoomed with it; Mr. Meredith brought out *Better Homes & Gardens* in 1924 and continued his career in politics, receiving nearly 200 votes for the Presidential nomination at the 1924 National Democratic Convention. He died, untimely, in 1928 at the age of 51. He was a leader of vision and enthusiasm, whose life-dream is realized today by these leading magazines, recently given a special award by the School of Journalism of the State University of Iowa for the attainment, through the years, of the highest publishing standards. #

Colonial advertisers used illustrations to stress identity. Daniel King, brass-founder and brand-maker, headed his ads with a brass bell.

How advertising helped newspapers support the American Revolution

Without newspapers, there would have been no American Revolution—and without advertising there would have been no newspapers. That's the opinion of Frederic B. Farrar, historian and newspaper advertising salesman. Mr. Farrar is senior vp-director of marketing and sales for Cresmer, Woodward, O'Mara & Ormsbee, newspaper representative. He is also a member of the American Antiquarian Society, elected in October, 1975, the same year in which he received his master's degree in history from Adelphi University.

■ As an historian, Mr. Farrar's special field of interest is newspapers. His master's thesis dealt with their role in the American Revolution. Its title: "This Common Channel to Independence: 1759-1776." As an historian, he has also put together a packet of reproductions of American newspapers, titled "Revolution and Newspapers: 1759-1789," which he is distributing to schools in an effort to spur the teaching of history. Thus far some 20,000 have been distributed, mainly at cost. Mr. Farrar's technique is to interest a local newspaper in buying the packet and reselling it to the schools. The

FREDERIC B. FARRAR

packet tells the story of the Revolution as it appeared in the newspapers of the day. But in addition to the news, there was advertising—often on the first page—and averaging something like 20% to 30% of the total space in the paper.

Without this advertising revenue the

newspapers which flourished at the time of the Revolution could not have survived, Mr. Farrar stressed. As it was, the newspapers played a crucial role in crystalizing colonial opposition to such grievances as the Stamp Act. And their accounts of the acts of resistance marked and spurred the developing rebellion.

■ For the most part, the newspapers in the colonies, up to and during the revolution, were weeklies—a few appeared two or three times a week. The first successful daily newspaper in America, the *Pennsylvania Packet & Daily Advertiser*, started in 1784. But without advertising, there could have been no dailies at all. The reason, according to Mr. Farrar, was technology. It took 13 hours for the printing ink to dry. So printing both sides of each sheet of paper would have required more than a day of drying time alone—plus the time to set type, print and distribute. The solution: First print the ads and then print the news on the other side—the day before publication. And since pages one and four were printed first, the hot news items ran inside.

For the most part, advertisers during

Much colonial advertising was for health and beauty aids. For example, in 1767, druggist Nathaniel Tweedy offered a "large and universal Assortment of Drugs and Medicines, which, as usual, he will sell on the most reasonable terms . . ."

the Revolutionary period merely listed their wares or their services. But selling copy began to be used, too. Among the first to "sell" was James Rivington, a retailer who operated a chain of three stores in Philadelphia, New York and Boston. Such early advertisers seem to have understood the need to repeat the message, since many advertisers ran the same ad more than once. An analysis of Philadelphia newspaper ads during the Revolution, for example, showed half the ads ran twice, 15% ran four times. #

How newspapers' ad column started

BY LAWRENCE M. HUGHES

Before April 1, 1926, there was no such thing as an advertising news column in any American paper. The happenings in the $2 billion-a-year industry were mostly ignored.

But on that date I started the first daily column of advertising news—in the 125-year-old *New York Evening Post*. It was not my idea. It stemmed from adman Earnest Elmo Calkins, Cyrus H. K. Curtis and, indirectly, Edward W. Bok.

Mr. Bok had long been editor of the *Ladies' Home Journal* and he was a son-in-law of Mr. Curtis, the publisher of the *Journal*, who had built a $200,000,000 fortune—mainly from advertising. In 1923, the Bok Foundation established the Harvard Awards for "good advertising," including a gold medal for "distinguished services." The first medal went to the National Vigilance Committee (now the Better Business Bureaus), and the 1925 medal was awarded to Mr. Calkins of Calkins & Holden, an agency which based its decisions on "truth and good taste in advertising."

Mr. Calkins, noting that some metropolitan daily newspapers already employed reporters specializing in such areas as real estate and insurance, concluded that advertising should get equal consideration. So he proposed an ad news column to Adolph S. Ochs of the *New York Times*. But Mr. Ochs didn't see any merit in the proposal (not for eight years, anyway). So Mr. Calkins turned to Cyrus Curtis, publisher of *Country Gentleman* and *The Saturday Evening Post,* as well as the *Ladies' Home Journal,* who had acquired both the *Philadelphia North American* and the *New York Evening Post,* and was finding that dailies can lose money fast.

Among a dozen New York City dailies, the *Post's* 35,000 circulation was the smallest. Its approach was conservative, its emphasis financial. It was read by the Morgans and the Du Ponts, the city's aristocrats. But how many of them bought in Macy's or Gimbel's or at other *Post* advertisers?

Meantime, I was 26 and had already

(Lawrence Hughes is marketing editor of Air Transport World. For five years, around World War II, he was executive editor of Advertising Age.)

been through several careers. Wanting to become a newspaper editor, I'd spent years with the Associated Press in San Francisco. Later, I got a job with the *Sacramento Union*, the oldest daily west of the Rockies. Then, learning that advertising copywriters earned lots of money, I got as close to that field as I could. I landed the job of publications editor of the Associated Advertising Clubs, in New York. And later came a copywriting opportunity with Campbell-Ewald's New York office.

■ Campbell-Ewald had the Chevrolet and Buick accounts, but I worked on Hyatt bearings and Howard watches—on which I did all right—and on a textile-tinter called Paintex—on which I did not do well. Came the day I was unemployed, I wrote to every big newspaper between Boston and Washington and got but one reply—from the *New York Evening Post*, where my immediate boss was financial editor Paul W. Garrett. He subsequently became vp in charge of public relations for General Motors.

So, in 1926, in a rickety building on Vesey St., I sat down to fill a column of advertising news each day in the *Post*. And things went slowly. I would phone the few people I knew in advertising and some I didn't know, and I sent letters to about 300 advertisers, agencies and media. But the letters didn't seem to do much good. The advertising business in those days was divided between those who had news to impart but who would rather keep it quiet, and those who were short on news but long on self-aggrandizement.

When 'Printers' Ink' Was It

Already, a dozen magazines covered the ad business and related fields. The one which mattered most was a pocket-size weekly named *Printers' Ink,* the bible of the business. Whoever wanted to spread the word about winning a new account was glad to settle for a couple of lines at the bottom of some windy *PI* how-to-do-it piece.

Now and then, facing the need to fill a long column, I'd go to see an ex-*Printers' Ink* man, Fred Kendall of *Advertising & Selling Fortnightly* and, in his off-week, borrow some press releases. And I'd do some sleuthing on my own. Early on I heard that the Pennsylvania Railroad was about to resume advertising after a ten-year hiatus. I heard that it planned to spend $500,000 through the J. Walter Thompson Co. And when neither the railroad nor Stanley Resor, head man at JWT, would talk, I turned to Ivy Lee, the famed pr counsel who had already sanitized John D. Rockefeller, and who was now handling the Penn account. I got six sticks of copy from him.

Questioning Woman's Virtue

In a news pinch, there were always the associations. They met fairly frequently and elected officers, adopted res-olutions and sounded off about developments in the field. There were the newspapers' Bureau of Advertising, the Periodical Publishers Assn., the 14-year-old Assn. of National Advertisers and the younger American Assn. of Advertising Agencies.

James O'Shaughnessy of the Four A's had been a newsman and a promoter since the Chicago Exposition of 1893. He worried about me. Once, when I'd done a piece about a Harvard professor's doubts about the agencies' 15% paid-by-media commission system, Jim was hurt. "Michael," said he, "this is just like questioning a married woman's virtue."

Bruce Barton Was News

I was to get a lot of copy out of virtue. For example, a bouncy redhead named Bruce Barton wrote "The Man Nobody Knows" and, on the strength of being God's press agent, as it were, gained for his agency the institutional accounts of both General Electric and General Motors. At a Four A's annual meeting in Washington, I sat in awe before Calvin Coolidge, who said, "Advertising ministers to the spiritual side of trade ... A great power has been entrusted to your keeping, which charges you with inspiring and ennobling the commercial world ... "

■ In New York, financial editor Paul Garrett would see me off on a 5¢ subway ride uptown to the Advertising Club, where I'd get a free lunch and hear a speech by Sir Thomas Lipton or Capt. Richard E. Byrd or whatever celebrity that club member Grover Whalen could snare. And Garrett was probably thinking all the time, "What a sinecure he has —and with $60 a week, too!"

I left the *Post* after 19 months to take a $90-a-week job on *Advertisers' Weekly,* which Bill Bros. was soon to merge into *Sales Management.* The *Post* ad news column was handled for the next six years by Herbert L. Stephen. In December, 1933, the *Post* was sold to David Stern of the *Philadelphia Record,* who dropped the column. Stephen moved over to *Printers' Ink.*

■ In the same week that the *Post's* column was folded, I began an advertising news column in the *New York Sun,* a feature which I edited for more than ten years.

Within a year, the *New York Herald Tribune* started publishing an ad column, written by Harvey Runner. Then the *New York Times* started one, under William J. Enright. Subsequently, the *World-Telegram* and the *Journal-American* also instituted advertising news columns. Meanwhile, in January, 1930, G. D. Crain Jr. challenged both the Depression and *Printers' Ink* by starting ADVERTISING AGE. #

Advertising's impact on U.S.: What it did from 1776~1976

What has been the influence and effect of advertising on the nation in its first 200 years? It has provided an important link in building a society enjoying free speech and an economy offering the highest living standard. That is the consensus of economists, marketers, college professors and others, whose observations were solicited by Advertising Age and are presented here.

BY KATHARINE GRAHAM
Chairman of the Board
Washington Post Co., Washington

A press to be effective must be profitable. I share this concept with some of the country's early newspaper publishers, among them Benjamin Franklin.

One cannot separate the impact of advertising on the nation from the impact of American journalism itself. The old ads are such an integral part of the old papers. Like new ads, they convey the life style of their time. The American colonists bought calico. Today we buy polyester. They drank Bohea tea. We drink Coca-Cola. Newspapers then and now brought the marketplace to the reader, presented the newest products, and helped educate him or her on how to use them.

But the road from Bohea tea to Coca-Cola was circuitous and contained a few unexpected jolts. Profits from advertising and printing freed early publishers from sponsorship by the Colonial governments. Publishers then and now could and did choose to criticize.

That such criticism when true might not be libel was an historic precedent which had its beginnings in the trial and acquittal of John Peter Zenger on Aug. 4, 1735. A mock ad satirizing the royal high sheriff as an escaped four-ft-high monkey brought Mr. Zenger his first pre-arrest displeasure from authorities.

The nation's first dailies in the late 18th century were established to carry shipping news and importers' ads. Soon these commercial papers began to show their political stripes. Their success prepared the ground for today's newspapers.

Post-Revolution Americans learned from these early papers about their forming new government. They snapped up fresh editions, read them aloud in coffee houses and passed them carefully from reader to reader. These papers lived on revenue from their advertising and print shops.

The press educates, investigates and presents the news. It will fulfill these functions only so long as its advertising keeps it profitable.

BY PROF. VICTOR P. BUELL
Department of Marketing
University of Massachusetts

Amid the controversy that surrounds advertising we may overlook the contributions it has made to this land we call America. Let me mention four: A high living standard, freedom of choice, competition and a free press.

Our living standard derives from our mass production system. Mass production cannot exist without mass distribution, which in turn depends on mass advertising. This process has created a price/income ratio that enables most Americans to enjoy a living standard far above the basic necessities. Equally American is the freedom of choice as to

how we spend our income and develop our individual life styles. It is advertising's influence on how we spend our money that is the focus of much criticism. Yet I know of no critic who wants to forego his or her own freedom of choice.

Competition is a uniquely American development fostered by our anti-trust laws. Advertising encourages competition through widespread information on price, quality, features and service. One has only to look at each Thursday's newspaper for convincing evidence. Finally, advertising provides the financial underpinning for our news media, making possible a free press unfettered by government subsidy and control.

Advertising is an imperfect institution that likely will remain a subject of controversy. It should be subject to safeguards to prevent deception or threats to personal health and safety. But when my friends complain of their annoyance at advertising's pervasiveness or content I remind them that it is a price we pay for freedom of information and freedom of choice.

I am not unmindful of the problems created by a growing population and economy, but these problems will not be solved by the popular pastime of attack-

85

ing advertising. Occasionally, advertising needs to be looked at in terms of its contributions as well as its imperfections.

BY JAMES PLAYSTED WOOD
Author, "The Story of
Advertising," Springfield, Mass.

Advertising had attained perfection before the end of the 18th century. Dr. Samuel Johnson said so. George Washington advertised to sell 20,000 acres of western land and from Mount Vernon ordered "American Broad Cloths," which he had seen advertised in a New York newspaper, for a new suit. Paul Revere advertised the false teeth he made. It is a truism that eventually by creating mass consumption, advertising made American mass production possible. Advertising underwrites manufacturing industry just as it supports newspapers, national magazines (those that survive), radio and television.

Much contemporary advertising, particularly on television, is in execrable taste, viciously competitive, and, worse, boring. It looks and sounds like an endless series of vaudeville turns with featured film actors happily smirking and cavorting for gold and golden exposure.

Yet advertising has, after 200 years of extravagant use in the U. S., one basic virtue which makes its manifest blemishes bearable. In the late 19th and early 20th centuries it was deservedly castigated for its sins. Too much of it was fraudulent. Legislative coercion and protective self discipline accomplished needed and lasting reform. Advertising went honest.

It seems now perhaps the most honest form of public communication; sometimes the only honest form left. Advertising is an open and avowed attempt to persuade for the profit of the advertiser, who assumes responsibility for his product or service and what he claims for it.

Advertising does not pretend to altruism or disinterested objectivity.

In contract, we are bombarded by the ceaseless propaganda of politicians, government agencies, labor unions, corporations, organized charities, and countless special interest and pressure groups, each of these faceless bodies trying stridently to make us feel, think and act as it wishes. Distortions, accusations, counteraccusations, and the new muckraking have all helped to fix current public communication on a solid base of confusion and earned disbelief.

Advertising does not masquerade as fact, as liberalism or any popular fetish. With refreshing honesty, it announces frankly what it is and always has been. It is the age-old cry of the peddler Autolycus in "The Winter's Tale":

Come, buy of me, come buy, come buy;
Buy, lads, or else your lasses cry.

BY HAROLD W. McGRAW JR.
President, McGraw-Hill Inc.
New York

While there are those who tend to feel that advertising is an American invention, Samuel Johnson, commenting on the state of the art in England some 200 years ago, concluded that, "The trade of advertising is now so near to perfection that it is not easy to propose any improvements."

In defiance of Dr. Johnson's opinion, advertising continued to improve, and so much of that development occurred in this country that it is quite understandable to consider advertising as we know it today as a peculiarly American art. And that is no accident. Advertising made mass marketing possible and mass marketing is integral to the functioning of modern mass production; and mass production and the U. S. grew up together.

While that may seem somewhat obvious, another American characteristic which made possible the dramatic growth of advertising in this country may not be as immediately apparent. Between the town crier of 200 years ago and the relatively recent advent of radio and television, advertising was almost wholly dependent on the printed word. It follows that a nation committed to compulsory public education would provide the level of literacy necessary for advertising to grow.

Given this climate, it is not surprising that advertising has played such a decisive role in the American economy. The first "automatic" factory in America was built in 1791 by Samuel Slater, and a decade later saw the first advertising

agents selling space in newspapers in half a dozen cities to manufacturers who already realized that the only way to keep their factories going was to expand their markets.

Until after the Civil War, market expansion meant primarily geographical expansion. And while the railroads created the conditions for a truly national market, it was advertising that enabled manufacturers to make the most of it.

For the industrial advertiser, the natural medium was the business press. These publications, through their advertising as well as their editorial pages, have always been the business man's most important single source of external information. Indicative of the business man's hunger for information is the fact that a railroad magazine was being published in this country even before our first railroad began operating.

One hundred years ago, the editors of *American Machinist* were apologizing for the "crowded" condition of its advertising columns, a concern which grew out of the magazine's determination to be "preeminently a reading paper." Today we have long since learned how well advertising complements the information contained in a magazine's editorial columns. And in the intervening years that mutual recognition—by advertiser, publisher and reader—of the true value and significance of advertising to the business community has in turn provided the opportunities for advertising to prove its impact on the growth of a nation.

BY ANDREW HEISKELL
Chairman, Time Inc., New York

The role of advertising in the creation of a mass market has been widely recognized. Its concomitant role in forging a free press is no less important in and to our nation's history. For advertising has underwritten the country's vast information network, without which our democracy could not long exist.

The alternatives are either no press—which means an uninformed citizenry—or a subsidized press, supported by foundation or special interest, political party or monolithic government. Relying primarily on subsidy from any source would be terribly limiting. I am well aware of the limitations of party power in South America and no reader of AD-VERTISING AGE is unaware of the limitations of *Izvestia* or *Pravda*.

In the U.S., we have an almost incredible variety of news and a gamut of truth. That can be confusing because it requires people to sort out and evaluate their information, to think and form conclusions. That requirement, perhaps as much as the information itself, strengthens our democracy.

Advertisers, unlike political parties or dictatorships, seldom try to impose their

opinions on the press. In fact it is remarkable that advertisers exert so little influence on the media they so largely support. That is surely testament to the strength of our political system as well as to the good sense of the business/advertising community.

Another non-economic but important effect of advertising on our nation is in the area of esthetics. The average U. S. family has developed a greater openness to contemporary art, a taste for better design through exposure to advertising. Its influence is pervasive in both print and television. Creative advertising, in fact, has nourished our esthetic sense as surely as museums. Just as surely, advertising has made most of us far more cosmopolitan by giving us an appreciation of customs and products of many peoples from many lands.

BY JAMES E. DUFFY
President, ABC Television Network
New York

Without 200 years of freedom of speech, would we now celebrate the world's most successful democracy? Probably

not. Without 200 years of advertising, would we now participate in the world's most successful economy? Probably not.

As Adam Smith said about the time our nation was born, a market economy will not function without information. The information today is disseminated much faster and further than in the 18th century, but the principle remains the same.

Advertising helps the economy in a multitude of ways:

First, advertising speeds things up. We no longer have to wait years for the discovery of a better mousetrap to trickle across the country by word of mouth. We advertise, and the world begins to beat

its path to our door in a matter of moments. And, perhaps more importantly, advertising contributes greatly to the development of those better mousetraps. The competition is tough, and if the product does not satisfy, there is enough information available about many more to send buyers elsewhere.

Advertising awakens us to alternatives. We do not remain wed to the ways of our own immediate circle; we learn how things are in other places, and we can adopt those that suit us better. And advertising is an equalizer. Anyone, no matter how small or large, has the opportunity to announce his existence and demonstrate the worth of his wares to the world at large.

Our advertiser-supported free radio and television system contributes mightily to advertising's ability to do all these things.

Our economy has grown, and continues to grow. With this comes national security, domestic prosperity and an increasing standard of living and improved quality of life for everyone. Advertising spurs that growth and improvement. Without advertising, our record of accomplishments and achievements over these past 200 years would be far less impressive and we would all be the poorer.

BY ERNEST DICHTER, Ph.D.
President, Institute for
Motivational Research
Croton-on-Hudson, N. Y.

The pilgrims were very anxious to start life without any of the mistakes they had left behind. They wanted men to be equal, free and ready for a fresh start. Suppose, just suppose, they had also decided to forbid all forms of advertising and could have made it stick. At the stroke of midnight all identifying signs of the baker, the candlestick maker, would have had to disappear; no town criers, no competitive markets.

neon lights, an economy based on handmade products. The need for communication with the help of a common advertising English would never have developed. The packaging industry would still consist of making barrels from which the owner of the general store would ladle out flour, sugar, more or less dear, or pour from large containers milk, vinegar and cooking oil.

America would have become a land without advertising, the dream of many dreamers of a better world today. The first arrivals were similar dreamers and rebels. It is easy to suppose that in reexamining all that they had left behind,

all the immoral and sinful frivolities of the European courts and the wastefulness of their society could have been replaced in the new colonies by a clean, dew-fresh and uncontaminated way of life.

Not only would we not have neon lights, but we would still be living in a pre-industrial, purely agricultural society. Subsequent immigrants would have had no need for a common language. Advertising language, bad as it sometimes seems to us, would not have contributed to the more or less "united" states. Uniformity, starting with governmentally standardized merchandise, would have been the rule. Competition would not have been possible, thus no new products, no possibility of advertising improved products. Most importantly, we would have lacked the basic motivations for hard work which produced the conquest of the wilderness and the continuously developing and ever-growing levels of aspirations.

The pursuit of happiness consists of creative dissatisfaction and discontent and not in acquiescence in the status quo. Just suppose we would not have been lured by the fabulous stories of the land of unlimited opportunities. Most of us would not have arrived at these shores and helped to fulfill the advertised dream.

BY PROF. PHILIP NELSON
Department of Economics
State University of New York
at Binghamton, N.Y.

Advertising has been around for a long time: The shopkeeper's sign, the brand on a manufactured goods. These two forms of advertising typify the two important functions of commercial advertising. On the one hand, advertising permits a person with special tastes and needs to find the articles that can best satisfy those needs. On the other hand, advertising provides assurances of the reliability of products that all consumers are interested in.

By providing consumers this essential information advertising has made an important contribution to the quality of life in these United States. This information has made it possible for consumers to find the best quality goods in terms of their tastes; it has at the same time encouraged the development of higher-quality goods and more diversified goods to satisfy the diverse tastes of consumers.

While this contribution of advertising has been important throughout our hisory, it becomes progressively more impor-

tant as time goes on. Both the vast increase in kinds of goods and services available to consumers and the rate of new product introduction have produced an increasingly serious information problem for consumers—a problem that advertising has helped to alleviate materially.

BY PROF. VERNON FRYBURGER
Chairman, Department of Advertising,
Medill School of Journalism,
Northwestern University, Evanston, Ill.

The freedom to choose in the voting booth and the freedom to choose in the marketplace are logical extensions of the "decent respect to the opinions of mankind" held by the signers of the Declaration of Independence. Respect for the worth of the individual human being is at the heart of the American system of government. Respect for individual opinions is manifested in a free press and a free market. We in the U.S. assume that enlightened consumers are capable of acting in their self interest and ultimately in the national interest.

As a form of communication that respects individual opinions, advertising has contributed to our nation's economic growth, has financed a free press, and has reflected the aspirations of a free people.

We cannot isolate advertising's contribution to our economic well being, but we can be certain that the myriad of products and services available in the marketplace would not be there without advertising. The tremendous investments required for new product research and development would not have been made if advertising were not there to build vast markets quickly and efficiently. Consumer spending, upon which our economy is so dependent, would have lagged if advertising were not there to stimulate purchase. Our economy would have produced what some bureaucratic authority or-

dered instead of what individual consumers wanted if advertising were not there to present the many options offered in a free market system.

Perhaps most important is the by-product of advertising, a free press, a press that not only is free from government control but one that includes hundreds of radio and television stations for coverage of local and regional news, as well as hundreds of magazines appealing to every reader interest imaginable, as well as television and radio networks that let millions of Americans tune in on national and world events. The opportunity to express differing opinions is enhanced by a press that receives its economic support from so widespread and so diverse a base as advertising. When the press is free, not only free from government interference, but free to fulfill its high promise, a nation's people have the best chance to enjoy their "unalienable rights."

BY JOHN H. JOHNSON
President and Publisher
Johnson Publishing Co., Chicago

Two hundred years ago we "advertised" the birth of our nation with the shot that was heard around the world. We packaged our new republic in twin wrappers of liberty and justice, and labeled it the United States of America.

Advertising has had a great impact on the phenomenal growth of America. No other institution has done more to enhance our standard of living through the diffusion of ideas. From town crier to communications satellite, the goods and

services produced by free men and women have been offered in a free marketplace. Our national character is best mirrored in the marketplace and the American marketplace was born, bred and matured on advertising.

Advertising has been a major influence in bringing about the cultural unification of our country. A century ago, there were marked differences in the habits, customs and consumption patterns of various sections of our land. The influence of national advertising caused local preferences to yield to improved standardization of quality and services, made possible by American industry.

Advertising has taught the American people to expect, seek and prefer the best that our system of free enterprise can deliver. This has stimulated a steady rise in our national standards of tastes and preferences. After 200 years, American life and thought continues to widen and deepen as a result of national advertising.

The advertising industry has greatly enhanced America's ability to market its "know-how" through its genius of communication. Our communications industry, with the support of advertising, has brought us closer together. It has incited and directed ambition, enlightened careers, matured minds, and opened the doors to new ideas. Advertising has forged an intimate relationship in the fabric of our nation. It is part and parcel of our way of life.

The history of advertising coincides almost exactly with the history of American unity. It was during the middle of the 19th century that the old idea of a culturally segmented America gave way to the idea of a culturally unified America.

By the turn of the century, advertising agencies began to bloom. This marked the beginning of advertising as we know it today. Since then, the American people have relied upon advertising as the most acceptable source of new ideas about goods and services that make for better living.

BY JULES BACKMAN
Research Professor Emeritus
of Economics
New York University

The U.S. has achieved vast economic growth during its 200-year history—to levels of living undreamed of by the founding fathers or by their children or grandchildren. A continent, rich in resources and with a generally favorable climate, an expanding population dominated by a strong work ethic and a willingness to save part of its current output, friendly nations on our borders so that we have experienced war on our soil only twice, a stable governmental structure, major developments in science and technology, expanding educational opportunities, and, most important, a free enterprise system in which there has been the incentive to seek out opportunities and to reap rich rewards—these have been the ingredients which have made possible our economic growth.

There also have been many facilitating factors, including the development of a

national network of transportation and communication. Advertising has utilized the many channels of communication to facilitate bringing together buyers and sellers, an indispensable prerequisite for expanding volume.

This is a vast country. In our dynamic and complex economy there is a vital need for the consumer to be aware of new products, improvement in existing items, and the establishment of new companies.

Substantial numbers of new consumer products continually have flowed from our laboratories and factories and contributed significantly to our growth rate. Information concerning these new products has had to be disseminated to potential customers over a wide area, if companies were to be induced by potential sales to invest in the required plant and equipment.

Consumers had to be informed of where in their own communities wide varieties of goods were available, often at different prices. Employers seek workers, landlords seek tenants, homewowners seek buyers. All of these needs and many others have required the dissemination of information. This has been the role of advertising.

Viewed broadly, advertising has been an integral part of the production process, has helped to widen markets, and thus has contributed to our rising levels of living. Advertising also has provided an important tool of competition, and thus has contributed importantly to our competitive economy.

By successfully advertising, a company can expand demand for its products and, in turn, the level of production. As a result, it can realize greater economies of scale because the reductions in unit costs of production more than offset the increases due to advertising. On balance, the consumer has paid relatively lower prices for the expanded output. This has been the pattern throughout our history. The interaction of economic activity and advertising has contributed to economic growth—and it will continue to do so in the future.

BY ARNO H. JOHNSON
Former VP/Senior Economist
(Retired), J. Walter Thompson
Co., New York

Throughout our nation's history there has been a close relationship between economic growth and standard of living as measured by personal consumption of all goods and services. Personal consumption, representing 65% of our gross national product, is divided about like this: Durable goods 15%, non-durable goods 43% and services 42%.

The importance of the consumer and of advertising in creating and stimulating desires for better living standards is dramatically indicated by an analysis of the last 35 years (1941-1976) of our history versus the 165 years prior to World War II (1776-1941).

In the last 35 years we experienced:

• 92% of the total 200-year growth in standard living expenditures (72% of total "real growth" with inflation removed).

• 92% of the total 200-year growth in advertising expenditures (also 93% of GNP growth).

This close relationship of advertising to living standards and economic growth can hardly be discounted.

Population has increased since 1941, but the "real" per capita standard of living (corrected for inflation) has more

than doubled in spite of our self-induced heavy unemployment and pressure to subdue consumer demands.

Particularly since 1963 "excessive consumer buying" was considered a primary cause of inflation. I pointed out in ADVERTISING AGE (May 22, 1967) how this misconception was leading to dangerously high interest rates, taxes, government deficits and unemployment.

Rapid growth of our young labor force emphasizes need for stimulation of substantially more consumption and production in the next decade to provide jobs and livable incomes. Over 4,000,000 persons were born in America each year during the 11-year peak of our baby boom between 1953 and 1964 (present ages 12 to 23).

Advertising can increase consumer demand for improved living standards, including betterment of environment, health, education and security—the basis of a growing economy.

BY OTTO KLEPPNER
Author, "Advertising Procedure"

The United States began with 30 newspapers from colonial days, carrying "announcements" of local tradesmen. As the nation grew, so did the local newspapers, with local and out-of-town advertising. National advertising did not burst upon the country until the railroads opened the West, 100 years later. Along with people and freight, they carried magazines from whose advertising the West learned about such products as Quaker Oats, Heinz baked beans, Lipton's tea, Ivory Soap, Mennen's talcum powder, Kodak cameras. To this day national advertising is the showplace of the innovators of America's consumer products.

One of the inducements for people to risk time and money innovating products is the assurance that if they create something good, they can tell about it through advertising. To build a reputation and a business on an advertised, branded product, a marketer must maintain its quality. The more money spent on advertising, the more has to be spent on quality control.

A successful product will incite rivals to compete, usually by trying to improve on it. Because advertising quickly shows up any failure to keep ahead, it is a spur to the constant improvement of old products, and to the creation of new ones.

Advertising has been indispensable in creating the volume of sales needed for our mass production economy, which has brought down the cost of products for the consumer and has provided employment for millions. Advertising brings to the consumer at home a living panorama of choices among the latest products, along with insights into better living

standards. And what about the media which deliver the advertising, along with news of the world, enlightenment and entertainment? Without advertising most media could not survive. How would you like to live in a world without media, without advertising? What would America have been like without advertising?

BY MARSHALL McLUHAN
Director, Centre for Culture & Technology, University of Toronto

When I was to give a talk to some British advertisers a few years ago, I wanted to impress upon them some of the differences between British and North American attitudes to advertising. What came to mind right off was our unwillingness to permit advertising in theaters and movies and public places of recreation. The British, on the other hand, have no objections to putting ads in any, or all, of these places.

After the immediate occasion of my talk had passed, I continued to meditate on our dislike of having ads in movies and theaters. When I mentioned this to a group of students, one of them volunteered the observation: "We go out with our dates to be alone, and resent any intrusion on our privacy." Gradually, I formulated the hypothesis that: "North Americans go outside to be alone and inside to be social, whereas the rest of mankind tends to go outside to be social and goes home to be alone."

This amazing pattern, which stands in stark opposition to the habits of the non-North American world, is borne out by our acceptance of advertising in the home on radio and tv. The North American home is not a place of privacy, but British and Europeans, on the other hand, bitterly resent any such intrusion on their privacy at home. This attitude extends to the telephone, which is allowed to enter British and European homes as little and as inadequately as possible. North Americans, on the other hand, are beginning to accept the outside as social space to the degreee that they have become accustomed to having the outside in their sitting rooms, on tv.

There is a great and gradual change

taking place here which could affect the future of the motor car in America. The car is the supreme form of American privacy which can be experienced only when we go outside our homes. Of course, the British and European car performs no such function of privacy, and are built accordingly. I mention this matter of the car not just to support my observation about going outside to be alone, but because some motor car manufacturers had begun to use this observation which I have uttered in public places.

Has anybody ever thought of the trauma of having our telephone privacy interrupted by advertisements? Bell Telephone recently decided against the use of the video telephone when they discovered a deep American reluctance to use such an instrument. While we accept the intrusion of the telephone into our homes, we are not yet ready to venture out of our homes via video phone to participate in a social life. The same reason which would make the video phone unthinkable in North America would render it quite acceptable in other parts of the world.

BY C. H. SANDAGE
Professor of Advertising, Emeritus, University of Illinois, Champaign, Ill.

It is impossible to measure the extent to which advertising contributed to the growth and development of the U.S. during the past 200 years. There is strong evidence, however, that advertising provided a significant catalyst in creating an economy of abundance. This catalytic agent functioned to provide information to an increasingly dispersed population, as well as persuasion to stimulate consumers to expand their desires.

■ This combination of information dissemination and persuasion contributed greatly to the process of division of labor and specialization of function in economic production. This undoubtedly hastened the movement away from a household economy. It made it possible for the "Yankee trader" to expand his market to the entire nation. Of course, advertising was not the only force contributing to this development. Other important factors would include the network of long distance transportation, regional and national magazines, and the ever-present work ethic. But without advertising, these other factors would not have been sufficient to move the nation to a high plane of abundance.

■ For the most part, the impact of advertising on the nation during the past 200 years has been primarily of an economic nature. More recently, advertising has been providing both a social and political influence. The future may well see a substantial increase in the non-economic impact of advertising on society.

The most significant non-economic impact of advertising may well be its contribution in modernizing our freedom-of-speech heritage. Freedom of speech is a hollow freedom unless there is effective machinery for distributing speech to those one wishes to reach. Advertising provides such machinery. It permits any citizen, at a minimum cost, to have his ideas of a social, political or ideological

nature distributed widely. Recognition of this aspect may bring about total acceptance of freedom of access to the media for such advertising.

BY ERWIN D. CANHAM
Editor Emeritus, Christian Science Monitor, Boston

Advertising has played a tremendous part in the American experience, but it is a role that has changed greatly down through the years and is still changing.

Prior to about 1900, advertising was convenient and useful. Since then it has greatly stimulated the growth of the economy, increasing consumption steadily and massively.

For many years, advertising was cursed by blatant misrepresentation. The patent medicine era was typical. But early in this century, advertisers began the "truth in advertising" thrust, and a very considerable clean-up resulted. This was fortunate, for as the century advanced the techniques of advertising became ever more powerful. Had these been harnessed to fraud, the consequences would have been dismal.

As it was, exaggeration and misrepre-

sentation were advertising's worst enemies in the performance of its indispensable social function. Self control was of considerable help. But the law, and the threat of law, also intervened and advertising claims were policed with increasing severity. The consumer's movement has become very vigorous.

■ Without advertising, the American economy would have been a pale shadow of what it became. Without pressure to keep advertising honest, its role would have been self-weakened and perhaps destroyed. On the whole, I believe we have had the best of both worlds: A very powerful advertising function, serving consumer and producer, helping standards of living to rise, and yet somehow restrained beyond the point of absolute excess.

We are asking very serious questions these days about unlimited growth. Standards of quality, of common sense, of moderation are veing vocated. Some of these things are subjective—as is good taste—but the stability and social validity of advertising in the future requires above all the credibility which rests on integrity.

CLOROX　　　　　　　PILLSBURY

Have things changed in past 40 years? Only on surface

BY LARRY PLAPLER
Co-creative Director, Levine, Huntley, Schmidt, Plapler & Beaver, New York

In a way, the movies of the '30s are more entertaining today than they were in their day.

What was spectacular, romantic and exciting then is quaint and amusing now, if not downright laughable. People sure have changed in the past 40 years.

And take a look at the art deco craze. Today you pay an arm and a leg for what was a commonplace plate and vase of the '30s. Why? Because tastes and mentalities have changed so much in that short period that something 40 years old has become an antique.

Now let's look at advertising. We're talking to the same public that has under-

gone this incredible change in the past 40 years. So, of course, ads have changed—or have they?

Vat 69

Obviously you wouldn't see any guys like these in a liquor ad today. That would be old hat. But what you will see with great regularity is the same old approach with updated models. And unfortunately, an old-fashioned idea in a 1975 haircut is still an old-fashioned idea.

Packard

Cut out a picture of just about any of today's luxury cars and place it over the Packard in this ad. Look familiar? This approach is 40 years old. Perhaps it's time it retired.

Colgate

Back in 1934 this Colgate ad promised that a toothpaste can help you beat a traffic ticket. Well, advertising has come a long way since then. Now there are toothpastes that promise to change the entire course of your love life.

Pillsbury Flour

A slice of the 1930s life: The young housewife has a problem with her husband. A sympathetic friend tips her off about Pillsbury flour. The result is that two young lives were saved from ruin—thanks to Pillsbury.

Today you won't find this story in comics book form on the pages of magazines. Admen are much too sophisticated

VAT 69

PACKARD

for that. Today's slices of life are on television.

Clorox

A talking Clorox bottle with muscles might have been a new man in the life of a 1930s housewife. But by 1975, countless household products have given birth to countless muscular spokesmen. And unfortunately, today's housewife realizes the only muscles that are going to help her clean the house are her own.

■ In conclusion, the changes in advertising during the past 40 years have been largely superficial, and haven't kept pace with the changes of people.

We're saying exactly the same kind of things to an entirely different kind of person—a wary, sophisticated, skeptical human being. Which might be why today's consumer takes many of today's ads as lightly as he takes a 1930s movie.

It's time we realize that talking to today's consumer requires more than 1975 trappings. It requires 1975 thinking. #

COLGATE

Magazines:
'To stimulate a free people'

BY JOHN MACK CARTER
Editor, Good Housekeeping
New York

"I consider such easy vehicles of knowledge as more highly calculated than any other to preserve the liberty, stimulate the industry, and meliorate the morals of an enlightened and free people."

In 1788, a prominent American, a patriot, a shrewd pragmatist in commerce and finance, wrote the above words in praise of magazines. They were addressed to the editor of one of the first truly successful general interest magazines published in America.

The writer of that stately and perceptive commentary in 1788 was George Washington. It was addressed to Matthew Carey, editor of *American Museum*, one of the most celebrated and widely read of the early American magazines.

Mr. Carey had emigrated to the New World in 1784, fleeing his home town of Dublin, where he had just served a jail sentence for the publication of what he termed an "enthusiastic and violent" publication critical of British political policy in Ireland. He founded his American magazine in 1788, reared it to an articulate maturity, boasting one of the highest subscription lists then known, only to have his periodical founder and fail in 1792 because of rising production and labor costs and "difficulties" created by the new Post Office Act of that year, which made no provision for the transportation of magazines.

The American magazine industry dates back solidly as a communications force to as early as 1741. And many are the rogues and sainted citizens who have been named its geniuses and this country's heroes.

In this Bicentennial year of American history, a study of the history of magazines makes for fascinating reading. It is a fulsome course in American political science, commerce and industry, art, history and American literature. It is a saga rife with legendary Americans who made their mark with printer's ink—larger-than-life political activists like Thomas Paine, Paul Revere and Benjamin Franklin; autocratic, aristocratic magazine industrialists such as Cyrus H. K. Curtis, William Randolph Hearst and Henry Luce, and perceptive, feisty women like Sarah Josepha Hale, who turned in 1832 from a destitute widowhood in Boston to lay a foundation for the many successful women's magazines of the 20th century through her own successful *Ladies' Magazine* and, later, as the long-term editor of *Godey's Lady's Book*.

One of the most compelling links to today's world of publishing is the 200-year battle between the "magazinists" and the U. S. Postal Service. It has been a conflict of historic proportion, ignited by Benjamin Franklin, America's first Postmaster General. Add to the contra-

dictory Franklin mystique of rogue-of-the-first-order and stalwart citizen and patriot, these revealing remarks, found in Mott's "History of American Magazines":

"In America, postmasters frequently became the publishers of newspapers and franked their papers through the mails, or they sent out their home-town papers free even when published by others. The fact that the postmasters might send periodicals through the mails free or not at all, as they pleased, gave them great power over the press and led to discrimination against competitors and political opponents. Benjamin Franklin, who had been appointed Postmaster at Philadelphia in 1737, undoubtedly refused to allow his postriders to carry the first magazine published in America; but when his own competing magazine came out a little later, he must have franked it through the mails."

As an aside to this incident, which is supported by a lengthy note, the Mott chronicle provides another passage which strikes home hard for today's publishers: "For 50 years thereafter the various magazines either utilized the mails *gratis* or by means of small fees paid by the subscribers to postriders and postmasters (a practice legalized in the Ordinance of 1782), or else they devised local delivery

Magazines went to war during World War II, as their covers, bedecked with the U.S. flag, urged citizens to give support by buying war bonds.

systems of their own or made use of independent 'newscarriers'."

■ Among those prominent on magazine mastheads 200 years ago, citizen Tom Paine was a zealous and celebrated magazinist before being hailed as the inflammatory writer of political significance that earned his martyrdom. In this year of 1976, when the world marks the declaration of the International Decade of Women, as well as the Bicentennial anniversary of the U.S., it is interesting to note that the American magazine industry hails Mr. Paine also as the author of an article which has been referred to as "the earliest American plea for women." Mr. Paine's article, "An Occasional Letter on the Female Sex," appeared in April, 1775, in *The Pennsylvania Magazine,* which he edited for Robert Aitkin, having been hired as editor upon the recommendation of Benjamin Franklin.

History, as it is taught in most schools, also fails to note that magazines of the Revolutionary era turned up any number of patriots equally as eloquent in print as was Mr. Paine in stating the case for freedom. John Hancock's oration commemorating the Boston massacre, published in the March, 1774, issue of Isaiah Martin's *Royal American Magazine* (otherwise known as the *Universal Repository of Instruction and Amusement*), is considered by many students of literature to be as compelling a Revolutionary rallying document as Mr. Paine's "Common Sense," so recently employed by

Supporting the war effort, Life and Reader's Digest in 1945 used their covers to present inspirational messages to "a united people."

Oldest U.S. magazines

Some of America's oldest magazines are *The Saturday Evening Post* which traces its start to 1728, *Scientific American,* begun in 1845, *Harper's* 1850, *Atlantic* 1857, *The Nation* 1865, *Popular Science* 1872, and *Cosmopolitan* 1886.

President Ford as the backbone of his Bicentennial year State of the Union address.

■ Magazines contributed heavily to the American economy. Look at such enterprises as the Curtis Publishing Co., Crowell-Collier, Meredith, the Hearst Corp., Time Inc. and McGraw-Hill. Even in an era in which corporate taxes and personal income taxes were virtually unthought of, these publishing companies swelled the coffers of the national treasury. Millions have been in the direct employ of the magazine industry or earned their living in affiliated services. Indeed, without such vibrant publications as *The Saturday Evening Post,* Ladies' Home Journal, Good Housekeeping, Woman's

Home Companion, McCall's, Collier's and their latter-day cousins, *Time* and *Life,* the advertising industry might not be the giant it is today; for the satellite system of mammoth advertising agencies, research bureaus and most public relations companies came in the wake of modern-day magazines that first burst forth in the last decades of the 19th century.

■ But if the advertising industry gained its first real strength from magazines, it has repaid the favor over and over again, supporting and fattening literary and intellectual magazines that had little base money to sustain them. Advertising literally made possible the founding of many of the myriad weekly and monthly publications that have been published locally in the U.S. From 1719, when history says the first ad appeared in the *Weekly Mercury* in Philadelphia, magazines and advertising have sustained a strong relationship.

National advertising began in American magazines. This early coalition between the magazine and advertising industries originated most of the modern methods of the national and international distribution of the manufactured goods and products of this country, and magazines continue to be one of the chief supports of the national distribution and the mass sale of goods, services and products today.

Women's magazines provided the earli-

est, most resounding and the most easily documented sales impetus for the goods, services and products of the past century. And women's magazines continue to serve as accurate barometers for charting sales impact and product practicality of most goods and services. Admittedly, these magazines had their heyday in the first 50 years of this century—marked most significantly in the late '40s and early '50s when the primary women's magazines began to rack up guarantee figures in the multi-millions, including astronomical newsstand sales. Now, wom-

Oldest magazine in West

Sunset Magazine is 78 years old—the oldest popular magazine in the West. It started under the sponsorship of the Southern Pacific Railroad and it was named after the line's crack train, the Sunset Limited. The L. W. Lane family bought it in 1928 and changed its direction to that of "the magazine of western living."

en's magazines seem once more about to surge dramatically. Leaders like *Good Housekeeping, McCall's* and *Ladies' Home Journal* are evidencing renewed vitality, and some of the new magazines being published specifically for women are creating a new spirit of magazine development. The fever burning in women to express themselves more assertively seems to augur changes in current magazine concepts.

In addition to women's magazines of general interest, there is another segment of the modern magazine industry which continues to promise growth and innovation even in our nation's recent recessive atmosphere. This is categorized broadly as "special interest publications."

"Special interests" of the magazine-reading public today range from the pornographic to the profound. It is not uncommon to see displayed in tandem on the same newsstand publications which border on the vile and others which are purity itself. Here again history is being made by the magazine industry, for there is at issue in a number of courtrooms in this land the seemliness of the open display of the former, not to mention the legality of the actual open sale of hardcore magazines. "Freedom of the press," battled for diligently by the earliest magazines published in this country, is in for another interesting go-round prompted by magazines.

For a long time in the early years of the evolution and establishment of the United States of America, it was often noted that this country had no genuine literati—persons whose working hours were devoted to writing as a full-time profession. Contributors to colonial and early American magazines chiefly wrote only in their spare or leisure time. It was only a little over 100 years

A cover girl in 1910 looked like this, with hair up and a ribbon, on the cover of Good Housekeeping.

ago that full-time American writers—magazine contributors, particularly—began to emerge. Edgar Allan Poe and Louisa May Alcott are among the earliest. Thereafter, until the mid-'40s of this century, there was a plethora of full-time writing talent available to magazines of all kinds—Dorothy Parker, Booth Tarkington, Robert Benchley, Ham Garlin, Willa Cather, Jack London—to name some of the more gifted.

Today, however, there is some question about the diminishing quantity and quality of magazine contributors. Perhaps it is time to reinstate the vocation of "magazinist" to more professional status.

American magazines have had their critics on subjects other than the abilities or diversities of their contributors. Many editors and publishers have the scars to prove it. Undoubtedly, some criticism is justified. There is no question, however, that, whatever their shortcomings, magazines throughout the last 40 years have made a valuable contribution to this nation and will continue to hold a significant place in American history. In 1941, Frederich Lewis Allen, writing for "The Bulletin of the New York Public Library," offered this summation of their net worth:

"These innumerable magazines of ours appeal to—and satisfy—a tremendous and undying urge to get on, to escape from provincial limitations, to acquire a sense of taste and style and at least outward distinction, to widen the horizon, to become . . . in some degree, citizens of the world. In that sense, our American magazines, considered as a broad group, give us a very impressive exhibit of democracy in action."

George Washington said much the same thing in 1788. #

Since 1895, radio finds its niche in media world

BY MILES DAVID and KENNETH COSTA
Radio Advertising Bureau, New York

Modern radio broadcasting technology was born when Marconi invented the "wireless" in 1895. One of the first to entertain by wireless was Enrico Caruso, who in 1910 sang into a DeForest radio-phone and was heard by ships at sea. KCBS, San Francisco, was broadcasting a regular schedule of news and music by 1909.

The first commercially licensed station (as we would recognize it today) is generally considered to be KDKA in Pittsburgh, which went on the air in 1920 and carried the first Presidential election returns (Harding vs. Cox). The first promotion effort was made by a still-active user of radio: Joseph Horne department store, Pittsburgh, which took a newspaper ad to tell customers how "Victrola music played into the air over a wireless telephone was picked up by a wireless receiving station which was recently installed here for patrons interested in wireless experiments." They were selling amateur wireless sets for $10 and up.

Most historians consider 1922 as the beginning of radio in its modern sense. In that year, some 690 licenses were granted by the Department of Commerce (the Federal Communications Commission did not come along until 1934) and 104 stations were spread over 36 states. As 1922 drew to a close, some 400,000 radio sets were in use.

■ It cost money to set up and run a radio station, and it wasn't long before enterprising owners found a way to earn money with their facilities. Just who was the first radio advertiser? There are several claimants. Arthur B. Church used his wireless in Kansas City to "advertise" radio parts to fellow amateurs.

In 1919, Dr. Frank Conrad promoted a Pittsburgh music store on his experimental 8XK (the forerunner of KDKA) in return for free records to play. The Reies furniture store sponsored a musical program on WSBT, South Bend, Ind., on July 3, 1922, and a Queensborough Corp. apartment rental commercial was broad-

MILES DAVID

cast on WEAF, New York, on Aug. 28, 1922.

As the demand for the air time increased, the preemption was invented! On Nov. 15, 1926, the A&P consented to give up its time to allow the beginning of the first network, NBC Radio. Within a few years ABC, CBS and Mutual followed—and today the networks have over 2,500 affiliated stations.

Most early commercials were institutional, just a mention of the sponsor's name and product, and if local, the address. Since radio offered music as well as the spoken voice, it wasn't long before advertisers found a way to combine them in the singing commercial. The first musical commercial was a barber-shop ballad to the crispiness of Wheaties, first performed on WCCO, Minneapolis, in 1929; but there is a counterclaim for a Tasty Yeast jingle that is said to have been broadcast in 1925.

In the 1920s, two hours of evening time on WAAT in Newark sold for $35; two hours, five days a week, on KHJ, Los Angeles, from 8 p.m. to 10 p.m. was priced at $150 if the client was also an advertiser in the *Los Angeles Times*. Incidentally, the $50 paid by the Queensborough Corp. apartments for ten minutes on WEAF resulted in sales of $27,000. It was radio's first success story.

■ But there was some opposition to radio advertising. Competitive media sought to

ban radio advertising, but there was no ban against it. An April, 1922, issue of *Printers' Ink* said: "Any attempt to make the radio an advertising medium ... would, we think, prove positively offensive to great numbers of people. The family circle is not a public place, and advertising has no business intruding there unless it is invited." But radio continued to grow and by 1927 there were 7,000,000 sets in use and advertisers spent $4,000,000 to reach 26,000,000 listeners.

From the beginning, radio broadcasters moved toward a variety of entertainment forms, ranging from sponsored symphony orchestra concerts (the Los Angeles Philharmonic was on radio as early as October, 1924), to comedy programs (Amos 'n Andy dates to 1926, and the Happiness Boys to 1923). Quiz shows made their appearance in October, 1927, in Los Angeles. Sponsors became identified with programs: The "A&P Gypsies," "The Ipana Troubadours," "The Gold Dust Twins," "The Eveready Hours." In those days a sponsor really "owned" a program. There were no alternate sponsors or participations.

During the 1930s radio became a truly national medium as the networks expanded rapidly. Developments of this decade included the soap opera, which became the mainstay of daytime radio, and serious drama. In 1936, the Columbia Broadcasting System established the Columbia Workshop, an outlet for unknown writers to submit scripts for broadcast use. But perhaps the most significant event of the decade came on the night of Oct. 30, 1938, when the Mercury Theater broadcast H. G. Wells "War of the Worlds," with Orson Welles. So realistic was this broadcast that many listeners, already tense with news of impending war, actually believed the world was coming to an end. This is still quoted today as an example of radio's power to play on the "theater of the mind." No tv show or movie probably ever had such impact.

■ Radio news dates back to 1921, and just about every station set up a news department. The wire services quickly found a new outlet to distribute world and national news, and stations not only reported the news, but interpreted it. Leading political and economic commentators joined the networks. Radio commentators often borrowed material from newspapers, many of which sponsored radio broadcasts to enhance their own reputations. News on radio has grown enormously and a recent study found 52% of all adults turning to radio as their first source of news in the morning, more than any other medium.

In the 1930s radio grew from 612 stations serving 13,000,000 sets in 12,000,000 homes, to 814 stations serving 51,000,000 sets in 29,000,000 homes. Among the major developments of those years were the invention of fm radio (1935), the creation of the FCC (1934), the start of professional audience surveys by Price Waterhouse (1930) and Hooper (1934), and a Nielsen-type meter system devised by the Massachusetts Institute of Technology (1935).

As radio became more sophisticated, there came on the scene the station representative. In 1932 the first representatives were Free & Sleininger (now Peters, Griffin, Woodward) and Edward Petry & Co. Before the reps developed knowledge of their markets, it was often necessary for the advertiser, or his agency, to take a train to distant cities and negotiate his schedules directly with the stations involved. Spot radio has grown from a $15,000,000 business in 1935 to $422,-000,000 today.

■ People liked radio so much they wanted it available everywhere. So the car radio was born. In 1930 34,000 car radios were sold (at an average price of $88). In 1940 sales reached 1,700,000 (at an average price of $35) and by 1940, 7,500,000 automobiles boasted radios—27% of the cars on the road. Today 95% of the cars have radios. And somewhere along the way a radio salesman created the idea of drive time.

■ Meanwhile, the soap opera technique was adapted to commercials and the oldest known "slice-of-life" commercial is attributed to Young & Rubicam. This was for the old Spool Cotton Co., now Coats & Clark. Y&R employed a "Perils of Pauline" approach with the client's product saving the heroine in the nick of time. (Incidentally, Y&R was said to be the first agency to establish a full-time radio copy department.) One of the most famous jingles of all time went on the air in 1939. "Pepsi-Cola hits the spot, 12 full ounces, that's a lot . . ."

■ At the end of the 1930s, the world went to war. All America learned from radio about the attack on Pearl Harbor and radio carried the President's declaration of war on Japan. Stations became active

in war bond drives, recruitment activities, morale-boosting. Stations served as clearing houses to forward greetings to GIs overseas. President Roosevelt had become the first President to keep in touch with the American people via radio before World War II with his Fireside Chats. He

---

How soap opera began

Before becoming Dancer-Fitzgerald-Sample, the agency was called Blackett-Sample-Hummert, and Glen Sample was the man who dreamed up the soap opera, adapting a 1920s newspaper serial titled, "The Married Life of Helen and Warren," to radio use. His show was called "Betty & Bob," which was sponsored by Gold Medal flour, a product of the Washburn Crosby Co., now General Mills.

Mr. Sample also won Procter & Gamble's Oxydol at a time when the brand had lost half its business and was being outsold by an eight-to-one margin by Lever's Rinso. He developed the "Ma Perkins" radio program—which remained on the air nearly 30 years, helping to boost Oxydol's sales past those of Rinso.

---

continued his use of radio during the war.

■ But there was a lot more than war on American minds. We had "The Lone Ranger," "Captain Midnight," "Kay Kyser," "Mr. District Attorney," "Hen-ry! Henn-RY Ald-rich!!" Not to overlook the lively Latin rhythms of the Chiquita Banana song or "Be Happy—Go Lucky Strike!"

With the end of the war came a return to a peacetime economy, and business boomed. As the 1950s began, radio had grown to 2,819 stations serving 85,000,000 sets in 42,000,000 homes. And advertisers invested $450,000,000 annually in radio.

But now radio no longer had the airwaves to itself. Now there was a radio set with a picture tube. Tv was first a curiosity, but it grew rapidly in the early 1950s. As a result, some said that radio was dead. Television could provide all the entertainment, news and sports that people wanted.

Radio advertising volume actually declined a bit for one year, 1954, and was stymied short of the $500,000,000 mark until 1956.

But radio was not buried. Another electronic miracle came along to revolutionize radio and give it a vast new audience. This was the transistor, which in 1948 allowed radio to find a way to "go where you go." Television, with its bulky tubes and chassis, could not match portable radio. So easily movable radios grew from 1,368,000 in 1952 to annual sales of 17,000,000 to 20,000,000 units today. In

fact, some 40% of sets sold last year were portables.

Now, radio realized the way to go was toward the role of personal companion, not the household-oriented medium. New program formats and variations on older ones were developed. Radio became highly selective. While television's audience developed mostly in the evening, radio looked more to the daytime hours for its audiences. It found them in cars, in back yards, on beaches, in offices—all the places where tv could not go. Today adults average three hours, 22 minutes listening to radio, compared with three hours, 48 minutes with tv.

In the '50s radio began to stress more local involvement: Local news and community service, since television positioned itself as a national medium. To this day many communities do not have their own television stations, while there is at least one radio station in 1,875 different non-metropolitan communities, according to the FCC. Almost half the radio stations in America today are in non-metropolitan areas. This year, radio stations will do about $1.5 billion in local business—five times as much as they did in 1956.

During the turbulent 1960s, radio kept on growing. The radio set count doubled from 156,000,000 to 321,000,000, surpassing the total population.

The earliest attempt at all-news broadcasting was on KFAX in San Francisco in May, 1960. This was followed by XTRA a year later, serving Southern California. All news came to New York when WINS changed from contemporary music programing. Shortly thereafter, WCBS followed suit. All-news radio has since grown to nearly 75 outlets under the auspices of Group W, CBS, and NBC's NIS as well as stations operating independently.

■ Fm radio came of age in the 1960s, too. While it had been broadcasting for the previous 20 years, it was considered a medium for classical music. But as the medium grew it diversified until today fm stations program every format, and the distinction between am and fm is only one of technology. In the early 1960s, advertisers asked, "What is fm's penetration?" The answer: Fewer than 10% of households.

But growth was rapid, and by 1970 some 74% of U.S. households had fm. The station count grew from 815 in 1960 to 2,164 in 1970, and advertiser spending advanced from $9,400,000 to $84,900,000. Fm set sales skyrocketed from 2,000,000 in 1960 to 24,000,000 in 1970. Today there are 2,767 fm stations on the air. Almost 95% of homes have at least one fm set, and advertisers spent about $300,000,000 in fm last year.

■ The 1960s brought great strides in audience measurement. Gone was the idea of *homes* listening to radio, for homes didn't listen, people listened. The old technology did not keep up with the multiplicity of radio sets around the house, the car, the office. The old mechanical gadgetry was underestimating radio's audience. So the industry—RAB and NAB combined—undertook the now-classic ARMS I (All-Radio Methodology Study) in 1964 to determine which methods of audience measurement might truly reflect reality.

■ As a result, better ways of counting audience were developed. Advertisers now could have a better idea of what their dollars were delivering. Along with local market studies done by ARB, Pulse, Mediastat, Hooper, The Source, and others, a national measurement was developed. The national networks cooperated to develop the RADAR studies to replace the old Nielsen national homes-listening research based on meters too large to be attached to all the sets a household owned.

Radio today is bigger than ever. For 20 years there has been growth in audience, sets in use, stations on the air, and advertising expenditures. As for the future, radio seems slated to continue as an inseparable part of people's daily lives. And surely that can only mean continued growth. #

Baby medium, television grows up since 1940

BY ROGER D. RICE
President, Television Bureau
of Advertising, New York

In 25 years—one-eighth the time it took the U.S. to grow from 13 colonies to a world power—television became the nation's most powerful communications medium and a vitally important marketing tool for American business.

Television is a uniquely American contribution to world communications. Before its take-off point, in the late '40s, television was first a dream, then an experiment, but essentially dwarfed by its sister medium, radio. Television went from occasional experimental programs in the late '20s to frequent equally experimental ones in the mid-'30s. (Veteran performers still recall wearing hideous green makeup and purple lipstick and suffering from the intense heat.)

In 1939, NBC launched regular tv schedules from the New York World's Fair, and WTMJ-TV, Milwaukee, applied for the first commercial license. Soon after, CBS and the Allen B. Dumont Laboratories followed with regular schedules of their own. In July, 1941, the Federal Communications Commission approved commercial television and six tv stations offered programs (three in New York) while about 10,000 sets were in use.

■ World War II halted tv's early growth. Anticipating the war's end, half of the leading ad agencies by 1944 had developed television departments. That same year, Lowell Thomas was featured in an experimental newscast and Hugh Downs, seated at a desk piled high with blue Sunoco cans, delivered one of tv's earliest commercials.

With the coming of peace, tv sets tumbled off the assembly line and a period of explosive growth followed. In July, 1946, the FCC issued 24 new station licenses. Television became commercially viable.

Because of the initial high cost of sets, tavern owners were the first tv set buyers, and flocks of people watched wrestling, roller derbies, Morey Amsterdam, "Admiral Radio Variety Show," "The Lone

BY ROGER D. RICE

Ranger." WNBT (now WNBC-TV) made one of the early audience surveys and found the viewers per set (mostly at bars) ranged between 16 and 17!

By January, 1948, some 102,000 sets were in use—two-thirds of them in New York. By April, the number had more than doubled. The public's appetite for the new medium was becoming insatiable as these figures show:

● 7,400,000 sets were sold in 1950.

● 14,900,000 sets (of which 7,300,000 were in color) were sold in 1971.

● 1974 sets hit the altime high of 17,-400,000 (of which 10,100,000 were color).

During the early feverish period of growth, the living room became the "television room" and the "tv dinner" an accepted part of family life. A big event in 1946 was NBC's telecast of the Joe Louis-Billy Conn heavyweight championship bout. The *Washington Post*, later to become an important tv station owner, commented: "Television looks good for a 100-year run." The following year saw another first: Televising the opening of Congress. In May, "Kraft Theater," a weekly series of live hour-long dramas, started on NBC, and that summer CBS telecast a Brooklyn Dodgers-Cincinnati Reds baseball game using—

for the first time—a Zoomar lens.

Poker-faced Ed Sullivan began his weekly variety series the following year on CBS, attracting the biggest names in show business—and a long-term sponsor, Ford Motor Co. Milton Berle made his debut for Texaco the next year and "owned" the 8 to 9 p.m. time period on Tuesday for years. Like Texaco, the early network advertisers bought full-program sponsorship, a carry-over from radio. There was the "Colgate Comedy Hour," "General Electric Theater," "Gillette Cavalcade of Sports," "Camel News Caravan," and others. Again, as in radio, agencies produced the programs, contracting with the networks to carry them. A network's primary function in those days was to deliver its affiliated stations. Since network television had limited interconnections (mostly in the East and Midwest) programing originated largely from New York and Chicago. The rest of the country saw the shows via kinescope recordings.

Even by radio's standards, program costs were low. In 1940, the total cost for a weekly show was only $20,000. Berle's "Texaco Star Theater"—with a 75 rating—reached 750,000 of television's 1,000,000 homes. Texaco's tab was $15,000 weekly, plus time charges on 20 stations. A $1,-000,000 budget could buy a one-hour program for 39 weeks.

Between 1949 and '59 the cost of producing and transmitting shows rose by 500%, and then doubled between 1959 and '71. Despite the increasing costs, television attracted an ever-widening clientele because audiences grew faster than costs—and advertisers recognized the medium's tremendous impact.

■ Most early tv clients were carryovers from radio, many in the package goods field: Procter & Gamble, Lever, Colgate, General Foods. The big-ticket advertisers, who used radio sparingly, at first were equally cautious about television.

On the local level, department stores became tv's biggest client, many—like Wanamaker's in New York—opening studios on the premises. But the honey-

Milton Berle (right) was doing his thing in commercials for Texaco products on "Texaco Star Theater" on early television back in 1953. With him was ventriloquist Jimmy Nelson, his dummy and dog, Farfel.

moon was short lived. Department stores didn't understand the new medium or how to use it, and television didn't understand their specialized needs. Today we've come full circle. Department stores are now local television's fastest growing category.

As television grew in size, to become a truly national medium, advertisers changed their way of using it. A combination of increased costs and more sophisticated research insights resulted in a decline in program sponsorship. Many advertisers switched to alternate-week or co-sponsorship. By 1960, sole sponsorship was a rarity reserved for advertisers who underwrote "specials." They often aim their message at selective audiences. The association between client and program added prestige and a "gratitude factor" which was important to some clients (mostly industrial and big-ticket companies).

To the bulk of tv's advertisers, the philosophy of Procter & Gamble, tv's No. 1 client, made the most marketing sense. P&G's view was that reach is more important than frequency of message, and that the best way to do that is to get your message into as many different homes as possible. So P&G—and most other clients—bought minute announcements in a wide variety of programs.

Because television was so powerful an advertising medium, many advertisers, after careful testing, concluded that it was more efficient to use 30-second rather than 60-second messages. By 1971, the 30-second message passed the 60 in advertiser popularity. Today the 30-second message is the norm, and despite some efforts to cut the message length further, broadcasters are determined to hold the line.

From its earliest beginnings in the late '40s, television has enjoyed tremendous advertiser acceptance because:

● Results could be traced quickly—almost overnight, when the message and the product were presented excitingly.

● Television arrived when the U.S. economy was making enormous strides. How much each was responsible for the other is hard to say. But television's fast turnover of merchandise allowed business men to plow back ever-escalating profits.

● Unlike radio, there were not many tv stations in a market. The advertiser could reach the available tv homes with a minimum of stations.

● Most of tv's early growth was in the big metropolitan markets—just what advertisers wanted.

To anyone in the 1950s who doubted tv's ability to move merchandise, the as-

How tv makes difference

NEW YORK—From tv's earliest days, educators worried about a decline in reading because of the medium's popularity. Many felt reading would become a lost art. But the Television Bureau of Advertising reports that whenever television presents a classic, interest in the book booms. The most recent example, TvB said, occurred when ABC televised "Eleanor and Franklin," based on Joseph P. Lash's biography of the Roosevelts. A St. Louis county public library has 23 copies of the book, which till then were considered as so much dead wood. "Then in one day," a librarian said, "they were gone."

tounding success of Lestoil, the first heavy-duty liquid detergent, rated as a classic. Produced by an unknown firm in Holyoke, Mass., relying exclusively on spot tv, it moved from market to market, generating tremendous business. Its homey, live-action commercials cost less than $4,000 to produce, and in 1958, Lestoil bought $12,000,000 in tv time.

Locally hundreds of business men discovered tv as a new way of attracting customers. Banks, auto dealers and food, department and specialty stores learned by doing. Successes ranged from Jim Moran, who became the No. 1 Ford dealer through sponsoring tv programs in Chicago, to the Country Store in Burlington, Vt., which used a 60-second live commercial to promote the week's food specials.

The tv commercial was the vehicle through which business men, large and small, conveyed their appeals to the public. But rules for writing copy for this newest ad medium didn't necessarily carry over from other media. Top-notch print copywriters, for example, who had no problem adapting to radio, often were stumped by tv's combination of pictures and spoken words. Ad agencies went everywhere looking for new people, hiring such unlikely candidates as recruits from drama schools and unpublished playwrights to build their tv copy departments.

The earliest copy was prepared for "live stand-up spots," really radio commercials delivered in front of a camera. The announcer held the product in his hand, being careful not to cover up the brand name, and talked to the camera. Since he often couldn't remember 60 seconds of copy, he read "idiot cards," words

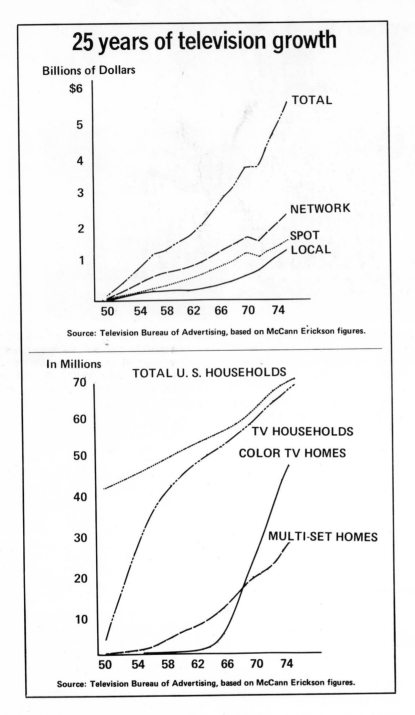

25 years of television growth

Billions of Dollars

TOTAL

NETWORK

SPOT

LOCAL

50 54 58 62 66 70 74

Source: Television Bureau of Advertising, based on McCann Erickson figures.

In Millions

TOTAL U. S. HOUSEHOLDS

TV HOUSEHOLDS

COLOR TV HOMES

MULTI-SET HOMES

50 54 58 62 66 70 74

Source: Television Bureau of Advertising, based on McCann Erickson figures.

---

printed on white boards that were off-camera. To add interest to the message, film slides and other graphics (balops, telops) were dropped in. The live commercial had the advantage of being inexpensive and lent a note of immediacy and believability that later commercials often lacked.

■ The live—via videotape—commercial continues on such personality-oriented programs as "Today," "Tonight" and ABC's "Good Morning America" (with Barbara Walters, Johnny Carson, Ed McMahon, David Hartman doing live pitches). An outstanding example of the truly live technique was a 1973 Sears, Roebuck spot for its Easy-1 power mowers which

highlighted the ease of starting the machine. The campaign was a great success despite an occasional non-start which lent credibility to the sales appeal.

Today, the live commercial continues to be available on many local programs where one of its strongest selling points is the live endorsement of the show's host or one of the 'regulars." (Except, of course, in children's programing or with over-the-counter drugs, where the NAB code forbids it.)

Although the live commercial satisfied the needs of some business men, others wanted more flexibility. Early kinescope recordings (aiming a motion picture at the face of the tv tube and recording it) avoided the live flubs but the

quality was noticeaby interior to live. Then film proved to be the answer. But in the late '40s, it took time to shoot, develop, edit, print. The equipment was slow, heavy and cumbersome and the commercials that were made were often slow, heavy and cumbersome. Because the camera lens was slow, movement was avoided as much as possible. This was a "live" commercial without much immediacy or believability. But time, patience and practice overcame many of the film's initial handicaps and it finally took center stage. The film cameraman and his crew could roam the world. Casts of thousands could be employed, if needed. All kinds of optical effects could be used to add interest. With a splicer, pieces of film could be blended into a masterpiece, supported by sound and music—and, later, color.

■ As filmed commercials became the norm in the '50s, "spot" or market-by-market television was a major beneficiary. For the first time, ad agencies could make low-cost 16mm film prints and send them to stations wherever they wanted to advertise. Thanks to film, spot advertisers could now control the quality of their tv commercials, a factor which spurred their use of spot television.

Still lacking, however, was the documentation of advertiser use of spot television. While expenditure figures· were available for network television, newspapers and magazines, spot television dollar activity was largely unrecorded. But starting in 1955, the TvB has issued quarterly and yearly reports on advertiser interest in the medium (in 1956 investments were $388,000,000, and in 1975 they were estimated at $1.7 billion).

If film proved a boon for spot television advertisers, availability of videotape in 1956 added another step in creating a "live" commercial without "live" handicaps. By electronically editing and recording both picture and sound on 2″ tape, the end product looked live and was ready for telecasting the same day, if necessary. Tape also allowed the user to correct mistakes as they happened. But there were drawbacks (no opticals, high cost of dubs) which took years to overcome before tape could challenge film's dominant role in the production of tv commercials.

Today, with a growing variety of portable, compact and relatively inexpensive equipment in both film and tape, the advertiser can pick from the three techniques—live, tape, film—whichever best services his needs.

Television has come a long way from the fledgling industry in 1949 which boasted about the medium's just under 1,000,000 tv homes and its $58,000,000 in advertiser investments, to a mature communications medium in 1976 with 69,-

Ed Sullivan was customarily a poker-faced emcee on his Sunday CBS-TV variety hour. But here he cracked a smile in a spot for Lincoln-Mercury.

600,000 homes, tv viewing per home topping six hours per day and advertiser investments hitting $5.9 billion.

■ Only by providing the public and the business community with a valuable service could this record have been achieved.

Without the hard work, perseverance (and sense of humor) of the early television pioneers, this would still be a dream rather than a reality of the Bicentennial year.

As to the future, Dick Pinkham, chairman of the executive committee at Ted Bates & Co., said it best: "Television is a sensationally effective marketing tool. I suspect we will be paying double the cost per thousand before the 1980s have been with us very long. And still television is a good buy." #

Business press traces its ancestry to colonies

BY CHARLES S. MILL
President, American Business Press, New York

Just as U. S. business and industry developed to its present massive and complex size from a tiny beginning in "cottage industry," so, too, did America's business press. In fact, all through the nation's business expansion, we see a parallel development—the growth of a specialized type of journalism which answered the need for education in the form of cooperative business knowledge, the free exchange of business information, the open discussion of common business, industrial and professional problems.

So woven into industrial development was the business press that there was actually a railroad publication before there was an operating steam railroad! The *American Rail-road Journal* (Fig. 1) made its initial appearance on Jan. 2, 1832 —although a typo in the issue changed the date to 1831. It is a direct ancestor of *Railway Age,* which is published today by the Simmons-Boardman Publishing Corp.

If, as business, industry and the professions grew, a method of business communication merely grew along with it, that would be neither surprising nor interesting. What is unusual is the acceptance of the business press as a vital part of the nation's business growth, indeed as a major contributor to it. From early days, business journals were not content only to report past history or current news. They carped, they criticized, they fought for changes in industry practice, yet they also taught, they explored, they made for themselves a position of leadership in the fields they served.

■ Three significant conditions account for this unusual position of the business press in the U.S. The first was that, from the beginning, Americans had a greed for print. They insisted on printed news. Nothing astonished foreign visitors more than the number of newspapers and the fact that everyone, not just the privileged few, read them. It was natural, then, for the average American to be attracted to reading about his business or

1. **Even before** a steam railroad operated, a railroad publication appeared—American Rail-road Journal (with hyphen!)—in early 1832.

his job.

The second condition which permitted the business press to develop into the primary communications vehicle for business information came with the demise of the apprentice system. Three forces arrived on scene at about the same time: (1) An absolutely explosive growth in the introduction of new invention, machinery, equipment and systems which revolutionized manufacturing and distribution; (2) the dissemination of the ideas of such pioneers of scientific management as Taylor, Gilbreth, Gantt and Halsey, and (3) an insatiable demand for education—for news of new developments.

This latter caused acceptance of the philosophy that to learn from others required an equal willingness to share information of new developments in one's own business. It is because American business men did adopt a belief in "cross-fertilization" of ideas that the business press could grow.

The third condition which one must understand to appreciate the unique role of the business press is that in the early

years of its development, few artisans, craftsmen or mechanics had very much formal education. To them, the trade publication substituted for the college classroom or the technical school. The editor readily accepted this role as "teacher of business." In today's world, the philosophy still applies—the editor thinks of himself as providing "postgraduate education of business."

■ America's business press traces its North American ancestry back to colonial days. The first publications devoted to supplying business information were called "price-currents," because that's what they did. They reported to colonial merchants current prices of imported goods as well as ship arrivals. The first of these was established in Halifax, Nova Scotia, in 1752. Another was started in Charleston in 1774 and still others in Philadelphia, Boston and New York between 1775 and 1815. From this tiny start grew the idea that business and porfessional men needed business journals to keep them up to date whatever their industry.

2. **In the 1840s,** coal and iron mining developed importantly, leading to launch of Engineering & Mining Journal, still publishing.

In many cases, the impetus for new publications was the development of whole new industries or the exploitation of natural resources. While elementary coal and iron mining were known in colonial days, for example, it was the developments of the 1840s which led to the establishment of outstanding mining journals. The rich deposits of the Lake Superior region were discovered at that time and soon after, the metal deposits of Nevada and California were opened up. Among the publications established in this period was *Engineering & Mining Journal*, still published by McGraw-Hill (Fig. 2).

The development of American business and industry can be traced by the founding dates of business journals: *The Hardware Man's Newspaper* in 1885 (which was the father of two Chilton Co. publications, *Iron Age* and *Hardware Age*); the first petroleum publications in the 1850s, and banking publications in the 1830s. Other publications founded before the Civil War included those serving such industries as shoe and leather, butchers, pharmacists, telegraphers and tobacco growers.

■ From the earliest days, manufacturers looked on the business press as a means of "getting their name before the business man" and publishers, in some cases reluctantly, accepted advertising income as a means of paying for expanding editorial service.

Records for continuous advertising abound in the business press. The front cover of the Jan. 2, 1896, issue of *Iron Age* shows such present advertisers as Jenkins Valves, Capewell and Bristol Co. (Fig. 3).

Most of the advertising in business publications in the 19th century was of the "tombstone" variety, consisting of little more than a few lines of type, sometimes an illustration of the product and the manufacturer's name. In a few cases,

Longtime users of business press

3. In 1896, the front cover of Iron Age ran industrial ads by such present-day advertisers as Jenkins Valves, Capewell and Bristol Co.

however, early evidences of selling in print could be seen. An 1895 ad in *Textile World* for Parks & Woolson Machine Co. proudly claimed that their product "Does the Work of Two Shears, Saves the Price of One Man, Saves One Half in Time." And in Vol. 1, No. of Penton's *Foundry*, published in 1892, W. A. Jones proudly maintained it was better to buy pulleys from Jones because "we can furnish you with them cheaper than you can make them," which sums it up pretty well.

Today about 70% of the average business publication's ads run in two or more colors, and spreads are as common as full pages. That was certainly not true of business publications—or, indeed, consumer magazines—in the 1800s. Most of them carried a multitude of ads on a single page. The *Iron Trade Review* (predecessor of Penton's *Industry Week* of today), sometimes had 24 ads on its front cover.

Somehow, the ingenuity and creativeness of the publishers along with the integrity and dedication of the editors—combined with the avid need of an expanding industry—brought the business press to the billion-dollar ad volume of today. #

What's ahead for admen, starting third 100 years

BY E. B. WEISS

Jim O'Gara, editor-at-large of ADVERTISING AGE, very fortunately did *not* ask me to attempt a profile of advertising in a remote future. Instead, he suggested I zero in on "What's ahead in advertising as we start our third hundred years." Therefore, I submit the profile of advertising that is just emerging in 1976—and which, in my opinion, will dominate advertising for the remaining 24 years of this century.

First and foremost, advertising will come under more and more sophisticated critical analysis by larger and more knowledgeable segments of our society than ever before in its history.

Second, advertising will come under increasing, tougher, more restrictive regulation each year of the remaining years of this century. (A rundown of the regulations controlling advertising as this century comes to a close would send many admen rushing to their shrinks.)

The questions that will be raised about advertising—especially by a cynical young generation—will include such shockers as: Is advertising essential? Does advertising result in better products? Does it raise our standard of living? Does it result in lower prices? Does it present a true picture of the product? Does too much of it insult the public's intelligence? Does advertising encourage the "wrong" type of consumption—for social status, fear, or ridicule? Do advertising pressures reduce entertainment (tv) to the lowest common denominator?

Does advertising create a "junk" culture? Tend to create monopolies? Reduce consumer choice because two or three brands preempt the market? Concentrate on persuasion rather than information? Is too much advertising in poor taste? Do ad budgets for "identical" products represent an excessive and unwanted cost to the public? Is advertising guilty of excessive invasion of the public's right to privacy?

■ Some advertising executives—perhaps many—derive comfort from their conclu-

sion that the new social pressures bedeviling advertising are merely a temporary phenomenun. The cold reality, however, is that society is evolving radical and long-term redefinition of the responsibilities of private enterprise. Politicians seem to be more acutely tuned into this social trend than some business executives.

Advertising, the most visual function of public enterprise, inevitably becomes a prime target in this sweep toward more social responsibility for private enterprise. Advertising functions in industry's most brilliantly lighted goldfish bowl. So advertising's philosophy must be more socially acceptable than almost any other facet of business. Unfortunately, it is not.

Industry equates "private" enterprise with "free" enterprise. But the public is saying that industry—and especially advertising—has abused its freedom. Moreover, it is obvious that in all advanced nations, free enterprise is waning (and in almost all Third World and Fourth World nations as well).

Industry may remain private nonetheless. But it will continue to lose still more of its traditional freedom. Advertising will, especially, again because it is so constantly visible to the public.

Can We Survive Self Regulation?

The fundamental question is whether advertising will succeed in regulating itself in the public interest, in the interest of the new, more knowledgeable, better educated, more skeptical public. If it does, advertising's future could not be rosier. If

it doesn't, advertising will be regulated down to the last period, the last image. That would add to advertising's already high cost in at least two ways:

1. Government regulation is *always* more costly than self regulation.

2. Government regulations will stifle advertising precisely as the Interstate Commerce Commission stifled the railroads (helped along by railroad executives who were just as short-sighted as some advertising people are today). Excessively regulated advertising cannot be adequately productive and that also means higher costs.

Will it be impossible for advertising to remain adequately persuasive under the new imperatives? Well, right now 85% of the advertising messages don't persuade because they are not seen or heard. Another 5% to 10%, although registering, are not believed.

So the advertising industry must ask itself: "Can advertising, under self regulation or imposed regulation, possibly achieve poorer results than most advertising produces right now?"

Could even dull informative advertising bomb more than so much presumably scintillating advertising does today—particularly in view of our new society?

■ In 1900 there were 12,000 engineers and scientists in the U.S. Today, about 500,000 scientists, over 1,000,000 engineers, and another 1,000,000 technicians are at work. Between 1980 and 1990 these figures may double. And between 1980 and 1985 instead of 7,000,000 attending college, campuses will be crowded with 11,000,000 students. For the first time, the large majority of teen agers will go through intermediate schools. Between 1980 and 1985, one-third to one-half of all young to lower middle-aged families will include one or more college graduates—many with masters and doctorates.

They will constitute the next mass market—affluent educated adults—first mass market of its kind, ever. They will control about 60% of discretionary income. Many will have been the campus activists of 1965-1970. They will constitute an intellectual and economic elite wielding a market power of enormous dimensions. And they will tend to be almost total skeptics with respect to advertising and marketing.

They will make a shambles of traditional advertising concepts because their education, their sophistication, will lead them into remarkable new life patterns. They will be demanding, demonstrative, articulate and cynical—especially about advertising.

■ Advertising has been keenly aware of the impact of the family's economic improvement. But advertising professionals seem to be only dimly aware of the increasing knowledge of important segments of our families—and even more dimly aware of what their higher intelligence, in combination with still more affluence, will signify in new life patterns.

If more advertising executives were keenly cognizant of the irresistible trend by the intelligent, affluent family toward eventual dominance of the marketplace—through its economic power, its intellectual power, its power as influentials—advertising would not continue to include so many programs, obviously aimed down to the lower, and even lowest levels of intelligence.

The Procter & Gamble advertising formula (depicting household drudges hailing the virtues of no ring around the collar), which has been so widely adopted and adapted, may have done more to bring about consumer legislation than all of consumerism's lunatic fringe.

Ads Misrepresent Society

Advertising had better beware of our on-coming "demonstration-oriented" society. The public—especially the elite segment I am pinpointing, which had ample campus experience with demonstrations—has become quite knowledgeable in planning and executing political and social demonstrations. Moronic advertising concepts will come under mounting waves of scorn, antagonism, forceful and even forcible opposition—and politicians will be quick to translate this into still more government regulation of advertising.

The toiletries and cosmetics business is one target of the woman's lib movement which charges that women are duped into buying beauty products for the wrong reasons. Co-eds on campus use practically no cosmetics—and somehow "make out" nonetheless. Feminists charge that tv commercials for household products portray housewives as creatures with infantile fantasies and a cleanliness neurosis. In advertising, they contend, a

Celebrating a centennial, Anheuser-Busch parades its beautiful Clydesdale team in a new flight of 30 and 60-second spots for Budweiser.

woman's life begins and ends with a clean wash, clean teeth, clean floors, clean breath and now a clean vagina.

Half the women in this country work. Yet, current advertising—especially on television—pictures them as stay-at-homes doing housework, taking care of children, giving their husbands pills for tummy ache, backache, or whatever ails them. Could a female profile of this type be more inaccurate today, not to mention 1980 or 1985?

Traditions Shattered

Should some household product marketing now be directed to men? Now that cars are designed and styled for women —and advertised to women—should more home goods, appliances, etc., be marketed to men as well as to women? The tradition that women are responsible for 85% of the buying for the home is being shattered. It was always an over-simplification. Will advertising now aim at a twin target—the couples who "share?" Isn't this a major part of the new consumer profile?

Obviously, we are about to kill off the mystique of both motherhood and parenthood. Motherhood, parenthood and advertising have had a close relationship for years. What happens to advertising appeals when this relationship is shattered? In that society, what is a wife—or a husband? And what is a family?

■ At this very moment, talented youngsters of high school and college age tend to read their underground publications primarily. They listen to underground radio. This is an extraordinary change that pulls the rug right out from under traditional advertising. Moreover, a sophisticated, more knowledgeable young con-

sumer will increasingly exercise individual taste. That individual taste will stem from their new social concepts. They will not tolerate fashion dictation or any other kind of dictation. They insist on doing their own thing; this is the clear message of their attire.

How do you advertise to a fantastically individualized society—to intelligent youngsters who fought for participatory democracy on campus and who are now carrying that battle cry into their business careers and even into legal careers? Theirs is to become a creative society. Creativity will be dispersed, fractionated. This is why Paris is dead. You see ample evidence in the current hunger for self-expression in their crafts.

How can advertising create status symbols as it had done for decades, in a society that spurns most of the traditional status symbols, including conspicuous consumption—that creates its own status symbols most of which are not relevant to possessions?

William Tyler, in one of his AD AGE columns reported that he served as moderator of a panel (of students and young married couples) devoted to advertising. Mr. Tyler showed them many ads. And in every case, he reported, the young people looked for the catch in the ad. Then it began to dawn on him that these young people were not doing this to impress him; they didn't do it angrily. "They did it without heat," Mr. Tyler said, "without rancor."

Even when Mr. Tyler showed his audience some ads which rated as good examples of truthful, straightforward advertising, he quickly discovered that it didn't make *any difference at all* to these young people. They still kept right on looking for the catch in every ad! Mr.

Tyler found this frightening. So should the entire advertising business—or its "third century" will not wind up with dynamic growth.

Ad-Government Partnership

Advertising cannot be expected to evolve and enforce its new social patterns without government participation. But it is still not too late for advertising to construct a new partnership with government to better serve the public and thus better serve the advertiser.

What modern society will now demand is that advertising must hew more closely to a moral and ethical line—not merely to legal guideposts. To date, the self-regulation score card in these new areas is hardly impressive.

I have referred several times to the vital need for advertising to observe good taste. Obviously, good taste is not a static social characteristic. Even five years ago, advertising of the new vaginal products would have been inconceivable. (Fifty years ago, Kotex advertising raised a storm.) So, changes in standards of taste can open new areas for advertising as well as close other areas.

Unfortunately, the current spate of corporate social responsibility advertising is hardly cause for optimism. The gap between corporate claim and corporate performance, with a few notable exceptions, is as sizable as the generation gap. And the total disregard in these campaigns for the corporate contribution to some of our major ecological problems has genuine Alice-in-Wonderland features.

■ Omitting the few exceptions, this is exploitation, not commitment. The young generation in particular realizes this and resents it. *The New Yorker* recently declared: "There is a youth-inspired revolution under way. It will not require violence to succeed. It cannot be successfully resisted by violence. It is spreading with amazing rapidity. Already our laws, institutions and social structure are changing as a consequence. Its ultimate creation could be a higher reason, a more human community, and a new and liberated individual . . . in time it may include not only youth, but the entire American people."

Why not? New social concepts no longer percolate exclusively down from old to young. Many now percolate *up*. This constitutes a remarkable reversal in life style that advertising cannot afford to ignore.

We are still a nation with a 12-year-old mentality. Most six-year-olds have one! That's why Harvard Business School, in one of its studies, found that five-year-olds are already cynical about tv commercials. How will advertising com-

Which Twin has the *Toni?*
(and which has the beauty shop permanent? See answer below)

Bernadette Fitzgerald of Chicago, the Toni Twin, says: "As soon as Sis saw what a soft, natural-looking wave I gave myself, she admitted I was the smarter half. Next time it'll be Toni for two."

See how easy it is to give yourself a lovely TONI Home Permanent for your date tonight

Soft, smooth, natural-looking curls and waves. Yes a Toni is truly lovely. But, before you try Toni, you will want to know—

Is TONI a real permanent?
Yes . . . it's the creme cold wave you give yourself at home. Like millions of women you'll say it's the loveliest permanent you've ever had.

Will TONI work on my hair?
Yes. Toni waves any kind of hair that will take a permanent, including gray, dyed, bleached or baby-fine hair.

Is it easy to do?
Easy as rolling your hair up on curlers. That's why every hour of the day another thousand women use Toni.

Will TONI save me time?
Definitely. The actual waving time is only 2 to 3 hours. And during that time you are free to do whatever you want.

How long will my TONI wave last?
Your Toni wave is guaranteed to last just as long as a $15 beauty shop permanent —or your money back.

How much will I save with TONI?
The Toni Home Permanent Kit with re-usable plastic curlers costs only $2 . . . with handy deluxe curlers only $1.25. The Toni Refill Kit complete except for curlers is just $1. (All prices plus tax. Prices slightly higher in Canada.)

Which is the Toni Twin?
Bernadette, the twin at the right, has the Toni. Ask for Toni today. On sale at all drug, notions or cosmetic counters.

Toni
HOME PERMANENT
THE CREME COLD WAVE

An alltime great in concept, execution and sales success was the "Which twin has the Toni?" campaign for the home permanent, which lured women out of beauty shops and into their boudoirs to wave their hair. This ad ran in 1947. Agency: Foote, Cone & Belding, Chicago.

municate with these young cynics as they mature? Certainly there is no reason to conclude that their cynicism with respect to advertising will automatically lessen as they mature. The contrary is more likely. This is one of advertising's great challenges in its "third century."

Tired of Inane Advertising

Yet the pace of social change has accelerated remarkably in all the advanced nations—even in some underdeveloped nations. Our society, and society in all advanced nations, has changed more in the last decade than in any previous two or three decades. There is every reason to conclude that this trend will continue to accelerate—and for at least several decades.

As one consequence, there is some evidence to suggest that more millions of consumers than ever before are impatient with advertising, tired of being treated like pawns in the marketplace, of being intellectually abused by a bombardment of inane and degrading advertising.

When 9,000 students from 177 univer-

sities and colleges were asked whether they considered advertising believable, a shocking 53% told the Four A's that they considered advertising believable only some of the time. Many of those students reported they seldom find advertising believable. That is hardly justification for complacency.

Certainly the more knowledgeable segments of our society increasingly question advertising's social contribution and economic contributions. These tend to be the very segments of our society that now control, or will ultimately control, the major slice of disposable income.

Restrictions, Restrictions

Ironically, label regulations may, in time, lead to more socially responsible advertising, because, as labels become more informative (which is, of course, a trend), they may achieve a higher credibility rating than media advertising. (In a few instances, this has already occurred in food advertising.)

Recently, Nabisco informed its managers: "Increasingly, customer inquiries require more than superficial response because one result of consumerism has been a drastic change in both the volume and nature of such inquiries." From the relatively simple "how, why and whatever became of?" letters of only a few years ago, today's queries are a great deal more sophisticated and cover a broadening range of technical subjects.

There is no doubt that attitudes of women to advertising as a social institution become less favorable as their educational levels rise. The co-eds coming out of college in the '70s and those who graduated after 1965 and will be extremely cynical about advertising. They are angrier about advertising than young men—and with good reason. Too often advertising still features women as sex objects, household drudges, second-class citizens, morons.

We are witnessing ⌐ many-sided revolt of individuals, especially young women, against the impersonal forces and institutions that dominate their lives. "Back to nature" and "the natural look" are potent current social trends reflecting that new social attitude. So is the wave of nostalgia that is currently true not only of the young generation, but increasingly true of the middle-age generations.

I conclude that, for the future: (1) any corporation of size must expect its free enterprise privileges to shrink at an accelerated pace; (2) the larger the share of market controlled by a corporation, the smaller its free enterprise privileges will tend to become, and (3) just as the public's right of privacy has been diminished, so will the corporate right of privacy diminish.

Those three basics of social accountability will be particularly applicable to larger advertisers.

Advertising that is not socially acceptable will tend to produce less return, will be more costly as a consequence. Apathy and boredom created by advertising are economic as well as social evils. The advertising business will become economically less able to justify ads that flagrantly disregard public time, convenience, privacy, sophistication.

The 'Aware' Generation

More advertising will be prepared with the realization that the young generation can't be conned as easily as its predecessors. This is the aware generation. It is not wise to forget that, or to defy it. It can't be conned in music, films, certainly not in advertising.

The increasingly fast pace of social change is obvious. Yet, while we are quite aware of this it is still startling to realize that:

1. The hippie sub-culture generation started only a bit over ten years ago. Yet it totally revolutionized not only our society, but worldwide society.

2. Modern women's lib took off almost exactly ten years ago. For the latest example of its power, note the remarkable changes in corporate maternity-leave privileges, and credit card and charge account liberation for women—both married and single.

3. The remarkable drop in the birth rate to the lowest point in our history started only about five years ago. (Like Sweden, our birth rate may drop below the death rate!)

4. The high divorce rate—it is already 50% in California for marriages seven years old—leaped ahead only five years ago. It has actually doubled in ten years. (This is one reason New York Life Insurance is now advertising life insurance to women.)

5. The enormous increase in the singles population—now climbing toward 50,000,-000—is a ten-year development. It constitutes a huge, distinctive segmented market. It is the spawning ground for more new life styles than the entire remainder of our population.

6. Consumerism, as a term, had not even been coined ten years ago. Now consumerism dominates marketing and advertising.

7. Ten years ago only half as many mothers of children under six years of age were gainfully employed. Employed mothers have tumbled traditions of the family.

8. Ten years ago the sexual revolution

A **famous slogan,** "The pause that refreshes," turned up in the ad above in 1929, while "Thirst knows no season" appeared in a 1922 ad.

had barely begun. One consequence: Johnson & Johnson has advertised a new type condom to *women*.

Employed women have particularly fierce time problems. Note the new devices that heat water for coffee almost instantly. Women are becoming increasingly important in product lines that traditionally were purchased almost exclusively by the male—autos, boats, major appliances, sports paraphernalia. Surely this suggests that the "masculine" era in still more traditionally masculine industries will now change rapidly.

Total corporate communication, including advertising, will now tend, in our large corporations, to come under the leadership of top executives, precisely as has been traditional with financial and operating programs. One reason is that in some large corporations the advertising budget is the corporation's largest expenditure.

In four to seven years, advertising's public, as well as the media for reaching that public, will have been restructured to an astonishing degree by remarkable advances in communication technology including satellite communication, the audio-visual tv cartridge, large dimension tv screens, etc.

The explosion of mass communication through the printed word started with Gutenberg about 1450, more than 500 years ago. About 60 years ago, David Sarnoff brought Marconi's wireless to world attention when he radioed the news of the *Lusitania's* sinking. That episode ushered in the era of electronic communication. Between 1960 and 1975, a 15-year span, mass communication technology innovated on a vastly more dynamic scale than over the preceding 500 years since Gutenberg first used movable type, and over the preceding 60

years of electronic communication!

Between 1976 and 2000, a 24-year span, satellite communication will change society more significantly worldwide than did all of the remarkable advances in electronic communication to date. The pace of communication innovation will show faster acceleration—and will involve still more sophisticated technology. The kinds of innovations in advertising necessitated by radio and television over several decades will now occur over several years—not decades. Further: Several innovations may be introduced practically simultaneously. And each could be of more monumental significance to advertising than radio-television combined.

The Agency Future

What's ahead for the advertising agency "as we start on our third hundred years?" As a quick overview of the future of the advertising agency of the future, I suggest the following:

● A number of large agencies will be accounting for up to 50% of net profit from diversification. Diversification will include both related services, semi-related services, and products and services not related to serving the advertising of clients.

● The fee system, in diverse forms, will come into increased use—rapidly.

● Extravagant license for creative people will be curtailed.

● The merger trend will accelerate.

● The house agency will emerge in new forms—more rapidly.

Clearly, traditional advertising-marketing relationships and functions of both client and agency are being daringly reexamined and are just starting to be daringly altered. In particular, the client is tending to take over some agency functions by using computers, and this trend may accelerate.

● The ad agency business is indeed in ferment. That state of ferment will boil still higher, and for some years to come. When it finally subsides, the agency of that era (about a decade or two hence) will bear little resemblance to its 1976 counterpart. The advertising agency of the future, although it may still be called an advertising agency, will no more resemble today's agency than the present-day variety chain resembles Frank Woolworth's five and dime.

That doesn't make the agency's future unique. Quite the contrary. Most consumer goods manufacturers point out that over 50% of their volume comes from products that did not exist ten years ago. Most consumer goods manufacturers—and retailers—have diversified into new business, new services. The ad agency, however, has tended to resist change. Between 1955 and 1975, agency change was on a minor scale, yet no two decades in history ever witnessed innovation on such a scale in most other segments of the economy.

Finally, the new communication technology (including satellite communication) will compel changes in agency-client relationships and functions. The next two decades will make the present pace of agency functional innovation appear to be a slow crawl!

■ The leading agencies of 1980-1990 will be vastly larger, more diversified, stronger financially, more profitable.

I note that when ADVERTISING AGE, in late 1975, convened a high level marketing-management panel to peer into the future, the panel members were unanimous in predicting that the traditional agency commission system is doomed. I fail to see how anyone could doubt it.

An increasing per cent of the budget may go into non-commissionable media. Cigaret advertisers already have moved in this direction. Toy advertisers may follow. Ad agencies may therefore decide to add new services on a full basis that will permit the agency profitably to service clients when clients divert larger slices of their ad budgets to non-commissionable media.

■ Client management is pushing for shorter timetables—especially on new products. And with good reasons: Competitors are unpredictable; product cycles are shorter; new products multiply. Agencies, house agencies, the various fractionated services—all will face rising legal costs due to consumerism regulations.

The basic philosophy for the advertising agency will therefore tend to include more flexibility and better financial control.

The computer will lead advertisers to take over more agency services. #